Grammar Galaxy

Mission Manual

Nebula

Melanie Wilson, Ph.D.

Dedicated to future guardians of Grammar Galaxy and to the glory of God.

Special thanks to my family, friends, and beta testers for their help in creating this mission manual. You're my favorite guardians.

ISBN: 978-0-9965703-1-2

Table of Contents

A Note to Teachers 1

Unit I: Adventures in Literature 2

Mission 1: The Importance of Reading 3

Mission 1: Update 14

Mission 2: Reading from Context 16

Mission 2: Update 22

Mission 3: Reading Comprehension 25

Mission 3: Update 31

Mission 4: Identifying Fiction & Nonfiction 33

Mission 4: Update 39

Mission 5: Story Elements 41

Mission 5: Update 47

Mission 6: Tall Tales 49

Mission 6: Update 55

Mission 7: Rhyming Words 57

Mission 7: Update 63

Literature Challenge 1 66

Literature Challenge 2 69

Unit II: Adventures in Vocabulary 72

Mission 8: Synonyms and Antonyms 73

Mission 8: Update 79

Mission 9: Vocabulary 81

Mission 9: Update 89

Mission 10: Fix the Prefixes 91

Mission 10: Update 97

Mission 11: Fix the Suffixes 99

Mission 11: Update 105
Mission 12: Superlatives 107
Mission 12: Update 113
Vocabulary Challenge 1 116
Vocabulary Challenge 2 119
Unit III: Adventures in Spelling 122
Mission 13: Alphabetizing 123
Mission 13: Update 129
Mission 14: Syllables 131
Mission 14: Update 137
Mission 15: Phonics 139
Mission 15: Update 145
Mission 16: Spelling with Phonics 147
Mission 16: Update 153
Mission 17: Compound Words 155
Mission 17: Update 161
Mission 18: Contractions 163
Mission 18: Update 169
Mission 19: Abbreviations 171
Mission 19: Update 177
Spelling Challenge 1 179
Spelling Challenge 2 182
Unit IV: Adventures in Grammar 185
Mission 20: Nouns 186
Mission 20: Update 193
Mission 21: Common and Proper Nouns 195
Mission 21: Update 201
Mission 22: Singular and Plural Nouns 203
Mission 22: Update 208

Mission 23: Pronouns 211
Mission 23: Update 216
Mission 24: Articles 218
Mission 24: Update 224
Mission 25: Adjectives 226
Mission 25: Update 233
Mission 26: Verbs 235
Mission 26: Update 242
Mission 27: Adverbs 244
Mission 27: Update 251
Mission 28: End Marks 253
Mission 28: Update 260
Mission 29: Quotation Marks 262
Mission 29: Update 268
Grammar Challenge 1 270
Grammar Challenge 2 273
Unit V: Adventures in Composition & Speaking 276
Mission 30: Handwriting 277
Mission 30: Update 287
Mission 31: Forms 288
Mission 31: Update 296
Mission 32: Thank-You Notes 297
Mission 32: Update 305
Mission 33: Directions 306
Mission 33: Update 313
Mission 34: Introductions 315
Mission 34: Update 322
Mission 35: Reading Aloud 323
Mission 35: Update 332

Mission 36: Storytelling 333

Mission 36: Update 340

Nebula Final Challenge 1 341

Nebula Final Challenge 2 344

A Note to Teachers

This isn't your average language arts workbook. In fact, it is a mission manual your young guardian will use to save Grammar Galaxy from the evil Gremlin. In other words, it's supposed to be fun!

Read the corresponding lesson in the *Grammar Galaxy: Adventures in Language Arts, Nebula* text to the student before completing each mission. You will then read each step of the mission to your student and give as much help in completing them as your student requires. It's important to note that most Nebula-level students aren't ready to work independently. Much of their enjoyment of their mission manuals will come from spending time with their teacher / parent.

Each step of a mission may be completed on separate days or all at once, depending on interest level and schedule. Missions are short so students stay motivated and have time to read and write in other ways they enjoy. Most missions ask students to use a highlighter to indicate their answers. Highlighters are more forgiving for students with less developed fine motor skills and are fun to use. Correction tape / fluid and adhesive flags will also be used for some missions.

Students will be asked to use vocabulary words in a sentence. Give students an example sentence first. All vocabulary words are taken from the text. Vocabulary will improve with repeated exposure. Don't worry if your student doesn't recall word meanings.

Missions marked "For Advanced Guardians Only" can be given to students who want to complete them as well as older students who are beginning with the Nebula level.

When all three steps of a mission are completed, read the Update to your student. For students who want more practice with a particular skill, be sure to check the website for resources at http://GrammarGalaxyBooks.com/Nebula.

To use Grammar Galaxy with more than one student, purchase a digital version of the workbook with copying rights for your family or purchase additional printed workbooks. Copying from the printed workbook is a violation of copyright. Thank you in advance for your integrity.

Have a question? Contact the author at grammargalaxybooks@gmail.com.

Unit I: Adventures in Literature

OFFICIAL GUARDIAN MAIL

Mission 1: The Importance of Reading

Dear young citizen of Grammar Galaxy,

Our father, the king, has recently alerted us to a serious situation that affects us all. We and other galaxy citizens have been spending more time playing video games and less time reading. As a result, our head librarian plans to stop buying books, words are dying on planet Vocabulary, letters are confused on planet Spelling, and poems, stories, and books are leaving planet Composition.

In order to save this galaxy, we need your help. We are making you fellow guardians and are giving you a mission to complete that we believe can fix the crisis. When you have completed each of the mission's three steps, you will receive a status update. We are counting on you!

Sincerely,

Kirk, Luke, and Ellen English

Guardians of Grammar Galaxy

☆ Step 1: Find Books You Would Like to Read

Write the titles of three of your favorite books on the lines (or have someone write them for you). *You can also print and tape pictures of the books from the Internet in the boxes below. You can use the titles of the books to help you find other books you are sure to like.*

My Favorite Books

1. ______________________________

2. ______________________________

3. ______________________________

Make a list of subjects you are interested in. *Circle the kinds of books you are most interested in reading below.*

science fiction

graphic novels

historical stories

fairy tales

real-life stories

modern fantasy

places

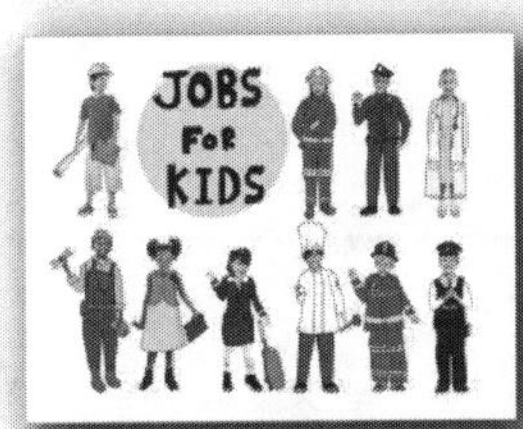

jobs

animals

people

history

science

sports

Draw or print and tape a picture of any other subjects you would like to read about in the boxes below:

Make a list of movies you love. *Many movies are based on books. The movie and the book are usually different enough that you would enjoy them both. Write their titles below or have someone write them for you.*

My Favorite Movies

1.____

2.____

3.____

Ask your friends, parents, and older siblings about books they love. *What are three books that have been recommended to you that sound interesting? Write the titles below or have someone write them for you.*

1.____

2.____

3.____

☆ Step 2: Check Out Books from the Library

Take this Mission Manual (that has your completed lists from Step 1) with you to the library. *It's a good idea to take a bag with you to hold your books too. Once you get to the library, you may want to ask a librarian to help you find books using the lists you made. Or ask your teacher/parent to help you use the search function of the library's catalog.* **Note:** *Continue to Step 3 if you can't go to the library today.*

Search for books on subjects that interest you or for recommended titles. *Your teacher or librarian can help you search for juvenile literature (meaning it is written for kids). When you are searching for books to check out, be sure to also look for an audio book or something that your teacher/parent can read to you. If you would like to check out digital books, ask your librarian to show you how. The more ways you read, the more likely we are to save the galaxy.*

Write the titles of books that are available on the lines below or get help writing. *Many books will also have call numbers that tell you where in the library they can be found. A call number may look like this one for the book, Polar Bears, authored by Molly Kolpin:*

J 599.786 Kolpin Molly

You may need to ask for help to locate the books you want. **Note:** *Your parent may want to purchase or borrow books for you if you do not have easy access to a library.*

1. ______________________________
Call Number or Location______________________

2. ______________________________
Call Number or Location______________________

3. ______________________________
Call Number or Location ______________________

4. ______________________________

Call Number of Location______________________

5. ______________________________

Call Number or Location ______________________

6. ______________________________

Call Number or Location ______________________

7. ______________________________

Call Number or Location ______________________

8. ______________________________

Call Number or Location ______________________

Check the books you find. *Once you find a book, skim through it to make sure it's what you thought it was. If you want a book to read to yourself, read one page of the book while holding up five fingers on one hand. If you come to a word you don't know, put one finger down. If you have five fingers down before you reach the end of the page, the book will be too hard for you to read alone, but someone could read it to you.*

Be sure to look at books on the shelf around the book you looked up as well. You may find other titles you would enjoy.

Circle the number in front of the titles that you decided to check out. *Write down any others you checked out below or have someone write them for you:*

☆ Step 3: Make Reading a Habit

Find a place for reading. *When you get home from the library, choose a place to keep the books where you are most likely to read (or listen to) them. Make it a place where they won't get mixed up with other books. Ask your parent to make a note on the calendar when the books are due. Also make sure you will be comfortable reading (or listening to) your books. If you are reading yourself, you will need a good light source.*

Where are you going to do most of your reading? (check one box)

- ☐ In your room
- ☐ In your family room
- ☐ In a school room or study area
- ☐ Other

____

Plan a time to read. *Aim to spend time reading every day. The best way to make reading a habit is to pair it with another habit you have. Reading before or after a meal or before bed every day is a great way to get reading time in.*

When do you plan to read? (check all the boxes that apply)

- ☐ Around breakfast
- ☐ Around lunch
- ☐ Around snack time
- ☐ Around dinner
- ☐ At bedtime
- ☐ Other

____

Keep track of your reading. *Use the monthly calendar on the next page. Write the name of the month (have your teacher or parent help you if you need it). Then color in a star for every day that you read. Reading for at least 30 minutes would be great, but even five minutes counts. Can you read every day for a week? Your teacher can print more copies of the calendar at http://GrammarGalaxyBooks.com/Nebula.*

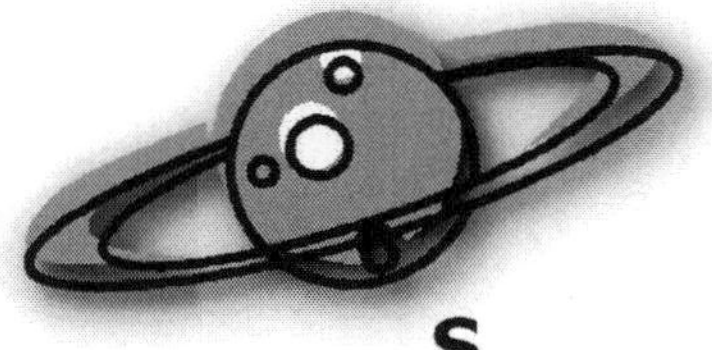

S	M	T	W	T	F	S

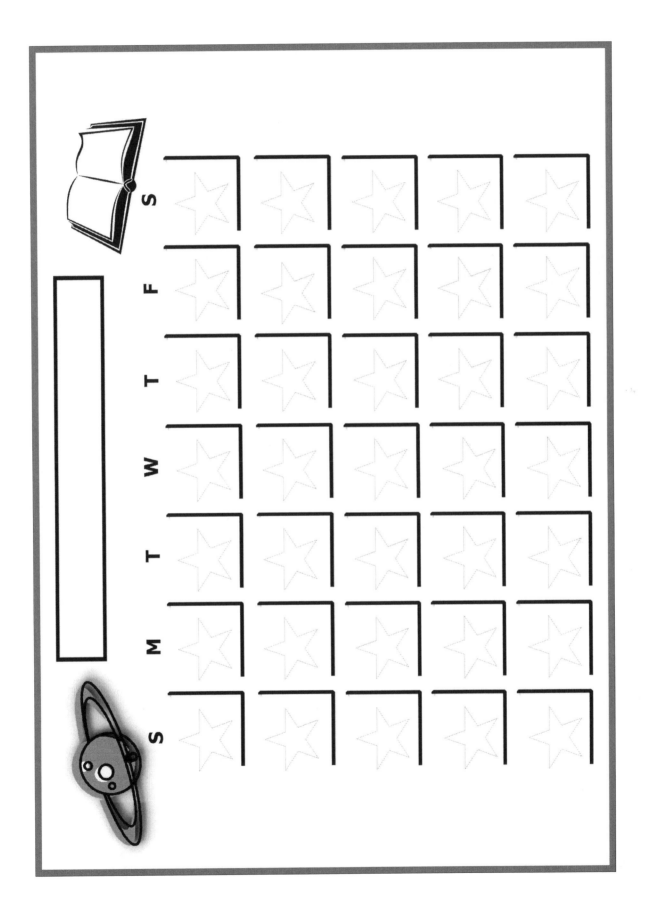

☆ Advanced Guardians Only

Use a reading-for-treasure map. *Discover the treasure to be found in reading by visiting each stop on your galaxy map on the next page and coloring in each direction as you complete it. You can read the next story in the Grammar Galaxy: Adventures in Language Arts, Nebula book while you are completing this advanced mission.*

Teacher's note: *You may wish to provide your student with a reward such as a new book for completing the map.*

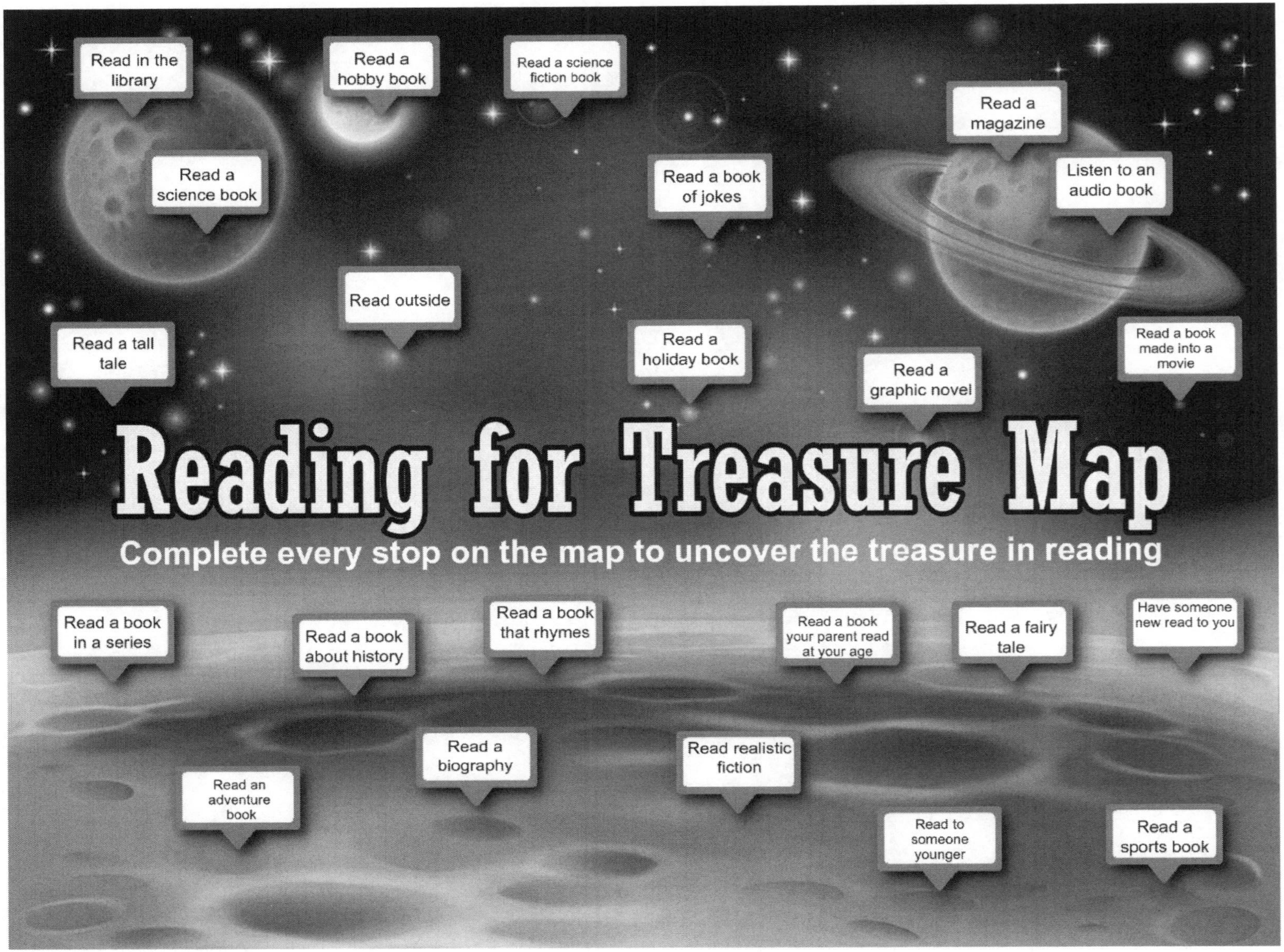
Read in the library
Read a hobby book
Read a science fiction book
Read a magazine
Read a science book
Read a book of jokes
Listen to an audio book
Read outside
Read a tall tale
Read a holiday book
Read a graphic novel
Read a book made into a movie
Reading for Treasure Map
Complete every stop on the map to uncover the treasure in reading
Read a book in a series
Read a book about history
Read a book that rhymes
Read a book your parent read at your age
Read a fairy tale
Have someone new read to you
Read an adventure book
Read a biography
Read realistic fiction
Read to someone younger
Read a sports book

OFFICIAL GUARDIAN MAIL

Mission 1: Update

Dear fellow guardian,

Thank you so much for being a reader! All over the planet, young citizens like you have been checking out books. The head librarian has had to order more to keep up with demand!

And we have more good news. Many words on planet Vocabulary are getting stronger because kids like you are reading them; the letters on planet Spelling are much less confused; and poems, stories, and books are staying on planet Composition.

In other words, we did it! We saved the galaxy from certain destruction and we're getting smarter. If you're like us, you've had a good time reading too.

We succeeded, but we can't stop reading or the same problems will return. If you are committed to keep reading so we can keep our galaxy strong, will you sign the pledge on the following page? Thanks again, friend. You're the best.

Sincerely,

Kirk, Luke, and Ellen English

Guardians of Grammar Galaxy

P.S. Can you say each of these vocabulary words in a sentence? Their meanings are given.

exquisite – *beautiful*

inestimable – *valuable*

tenacity – *determination*

composition – *writing*

Guardian of the Galaxy Pledge

I am committed to fulfilling my duties as a guardian of Grammar Galaxy, the most important of which is to read. I pledge to choose good books that I can read myself or have read to me. I will do my very best to read every day so I can learn, enjoy life, and keep the galaxy strong.

Signed,

____

Date:____________________________________

Note: *Put the date in this format M/D/YY using these numbers for the months. If today is January 4th, 2016, you would write 1/4/16. (Just put the last two digits of the year.)*

1-Jan 2-Feb 3-Mar 4-Apr 5-May 6-Jun 7-Jul 8-Aug 9-Sep 10-Oct 11-Nov 12-Dec

OFFICIAL GUARDIAN MAIL

Mission 2: Reading from Context

Dear guardian friends,

We have an urgent mission for you. Many homographs (words that are spelled the same way but have different meanings) have left planet Sentence. The problem this has created is we cannot use these words.

We need your help to determine which words are missing and where they belong. Working together, we can recover from this crisis. Thank you for being a reader and we will update you when your mission is complete.

Sincerely,

Kirk, Luke, and Ellen English

Guardians of Grammar Galaxy

P.S. Remember to color in the stars for reading each day! (P.S. stands for postscript or "after the writing.")

☆ Step 1: Stay On Guard & Use Pictures as Context

On Guard. Each mission we send you will have a series of questions to keep you on guard, prepared to protect the galaxy.

Use a highlighter to mark TRUE or FALSE for each question.

1. Planets Vocabulary and Spelling were two of the planets affected by too little reading in the galaxy. TRUE FALSE
2. One way to find books you will like is to look up subjects you are interested in. TRUE FALSE
3. One way to read more often is to plan a time to read. TRUE FALSE
4. A call number tells you the location of a book in the library. TRUE FALSE
5. The more you read, the smarter you will be. TRUE FALSE

Say each of these words in a sentence. *Their meanings are given.*

ecstatic – *thrilled* **fibbing** – *lying* **excursion** – *trip*

Use pictures as context to find and highlight the missing word. *Look at the picture and then use a highlighter to mark the word that belongs in the blank.*

1. When Johnny is upset, he likes to kick a __________ around.

rock iPod can

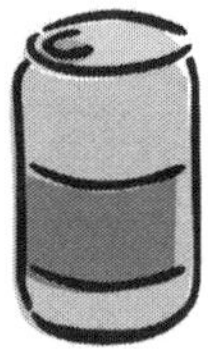

2. Jake flopped down on his____________ in the pool.

back face cat

3. Sam never plays with __________.

bugs matches toys

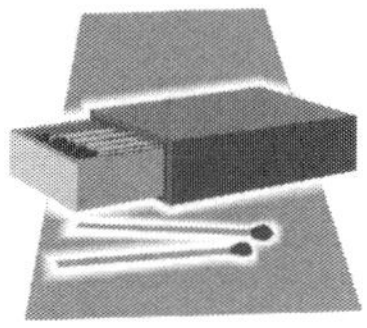

4. Please give the dog a bath in the __________.

sink tub shower

5. I'm not old enough to __________ the boat.

paint row build

☆ Step 2: Use Words as Context and Give Meanings of Homographs

Draw a line from each word to the sentence it belongs in. *Highlight the eye witness words in each sentence that are clues to the missing word. There may be more than one.*

Example: The football player ran the ball for a first ________.— down

1. I was just given a pen pal so I will write him a ___________.
2. Joe's baby brother loves to _____ good-bye.
3. Our mother told us to go play in the back _____.
4. It was time to _____ the candles on the birthday cake.
5. The little girl climbed the ladder, but couldn't get _____.

light

yard

wave

letter

down

Activity. *Try to tell your teacher at least two meanings for each of the homographs listed below.*

bank nail park rock mind

☆ Step 3: Matching and Identifying Homographs

Match the homographs. *Draw a line between two pictures that show different meanings of the same word.*

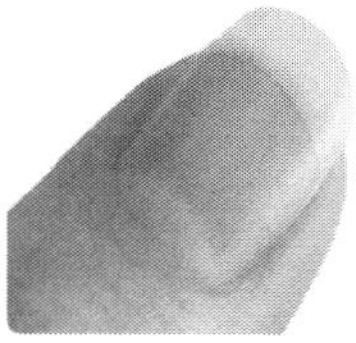

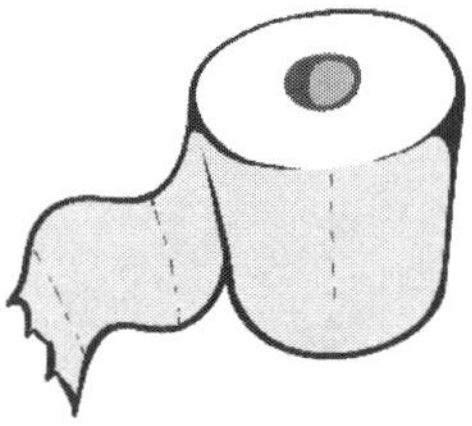

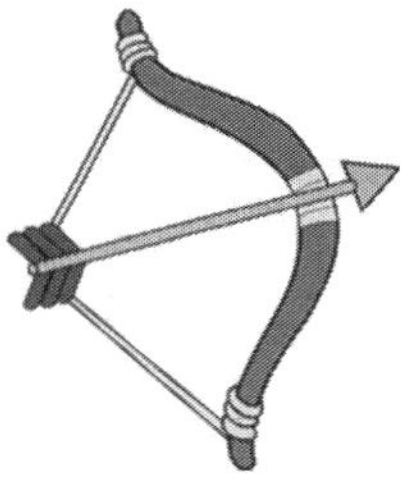

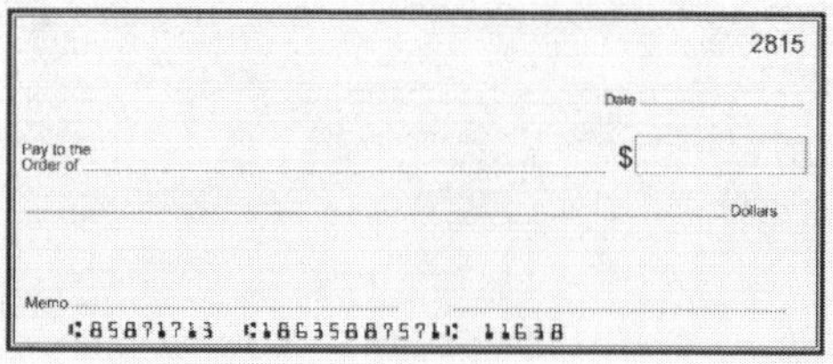

Vocabulary Victory! Do you remember what these words mean? *Look at Step 1 if you forgot.*

ecstatic **fibbing** **excursion**

☆ Advanced Guardians Only

Write a sentence using two meanings for the same homograph. For example, I had to light the candle when the light went out. *You can dictate (which means to say the sentence and have someone else write it for you) if you'd like.*

OFFICIAL GUARDIAN MAIL

Mission 2: Update

Dear amazing guardians,

We did it! Grammar Patrol brought the homographs' ship home to planet Sentence. Working together, we were able to determine where most of the missing words went and we're able to use them once again.

We are attaching the solutions to the homograph mysteries, so you know you didn't miss any. There are still a few homographs who haven't been returned to their sentences yet, so we will ask for your help with them in the future.

Sincerely,

Kirk, Luke, and Ellen English

Guardians of Grammar Galaxy

From the text

The king wanted to go for a walk; the word missing from Luke's book was fire.

Step 1 Solutions

On Guard.

1.	Planets Vocabulary and Spelling were two of the planets affected by too little reading in the galaxy.	TRUE FALSE
2.	One way to find books you will like is to look up subjects you are interested in.	TRUE FALSE
3.	One way to read more often is to plan a time to read.	TRUE FALSE
4.	A call number tells you the location of a book in the library.	TRUE FALSE
5.	The more you read, the smarter you will be.	TRUE FALSE

1. When Johnny is upset, he likes to kick a ___________ around.

rock iPod can

2. Jake flopped down on his____________ in the pool.

back face cat

3. Sam never plays with ___________.

bugs matches toys

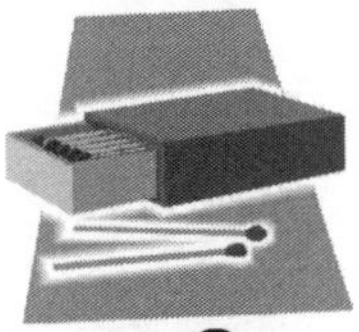

4. Please give the dog a bath in the ___________.

sink tub shower

5. I'm not old enough to ___________ the boat.

paint row build

Step 2 Solutions

Clue words may vary.

1. I was just given a pen pal so I will write him a letter.
2. Joe's baby brother loves to wave good-bye.
3. Our mother told us to go play in the back yard.
4. It was time to light the candles on the birthday cake.
5. The little girl climbed the ladder, but couldn't get down.

Step 3 Solutions

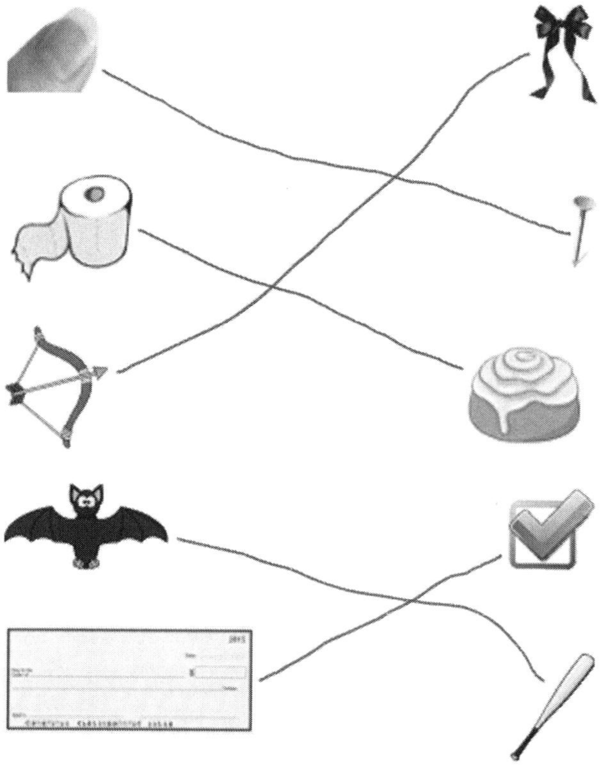

OFFICIAL GUARDIAN MAIL

Mission 3: Reading Comprehension

Dear fellow guardians,

Once again, we are in trouble. A phoneme karaoke contest in Phonics City has made our ability to understand what we read very difficult. We think we have the solution, but still need your help.

Please complete every step of the mission and you will get an update from us. And no matter what, don't stop reading!

Sincerely,

Kirk, Luke, and Ellen English

Guardians of Grammar Galaxy

☆ Step 1: Stay On Guard & Understanding What Happened

On Guard. *Use a highlighter to mark TRUE or FALSE for each statement.*

1. The less you read, the better you will be at spelling.	TRUE	FALSE
2. If you don't understand what you read, you need a haircut.	TRUE	FALSE
3. A phoneme is a long word.	TRUE	FALSE
4. A homograph is a word that sounds like your name.	TRUE	FALSE
5. You don't need to know phonics to understand what you read.	TRUE	FALSE

Say each of these words in a sentence. *Their meanings are given.*

dilemma – *problem* **phonemes** – *units of sound* **astounded** – *shocked*

Understanding What Happened. *Highlight the correct answer to each question.*

1. What couldn't Kirk understand?
   a. the plan b. the menu c. the weather forecast

2. At dinner, Ellen was distracted by her?
   a. communicator b. nails c. hair

3. Luke thought he knew _____ pretty well?
   a. phonics b. physics c. math

4. A phoneme is a:
   a. unit of sound b. word c. singing group

5. The English children went to _____ to stop the karaoke contest?
   a. Phonics City b. Mars c. the kitchen

☆ Step 2: Reading for Understanding

Read the following story and then answer the questions about it for your teacher. *Get help reading words you don't know.*

Ben had a dog named Bo. They lived on a farm. Bo did not like cats. One day Bo saw a cat and ran to get it. The cat ran and ran to the top of a barn. The cat jumped out of the top of the barn and fell far down. She was fine. Bo kept running after the cat. He could not stop. He fell far down and barked. He hit hard. He was fine but did not run to get cats after that.

1. To whom did Bo belong?
2. What pet did Bo not like?
3. Where did Ben and Bo live?
4. Why did Bo keep running after the cat at the top of the barn?
5. Why didn't Bo chase cats at the end of the story?

Activity. *Have your teacher read you a short story of your choice and ask you five questions about it. See if you can get them all correct.*

☆ Step 3: Reading Facts for Understanding

Read the following paragraph or have your teacher read it to you. *Answer the questions about it for your teacher. Put the number of the sentence in the blank that gives you the answer to the question. The first one is done for you.*

[1]Howler monkeys are very loud animals. [2]They howl in the morning and at night. [3]Males howl to keep their land from other males. [4]The more monkeys there are, the more they howl. [5]The sound can travel for three miles.

1. Howler monkeys are known for being very what? __1__ (loud)
2. What time of day do howler monkeys howl? ___
3. The more monkeys there are, the more they what? ___
4. One reason males howl is? ___
5. How far can the sound of a howling monkey travel? ___

Vocabulary Victory! Do you remember what these words mean? *Check Step 1 if you forgot.*

dilemma **phonemes** **astounded**

☆ Advanced Guardians Only

Write or dictate (say) a question that only someone who has read your favorite book could answer. *See if your teacher knows the answer.*

OFFICIAL GUARDIAN MAIL

Mission 3: Update

Dear trusted guardians,

Good news! Reading comprehension has improved across the galaxy. The karaoke contest was canceled and won't be rescheduled because the phonemes couldn't get along in groups. They are back to work at home.

We can't thank you enough for your help, but we ask you to be on your guard. When we do not understand what we read, we are all in trouble. We have asked teachers to keep checking that their students understand by asking questions. We know you'll cooperate so we can defeat the Gremlin!

We are attaching the answers to the questions we sent you. Until next time, happy reading!

Sincerely,

Kirk, Luke, and Ellen English

Guardians of Grammar Galaxy

Step 1 Solutions

On Guard.

1.	The less you read, the better you will be at spelling.	TRUE	FALSE
2.	If you don't understand what you read, you need a haircut.	TRUE	FALSE
3.	A phoneme is a long word.	TRUE	FALSE
4.	A homograph is a word that sounds like your name.	TRUE	FALSE
5.	You don't need to know phonics to understand what you read.	TRUE	FALSE

Understanding What Happened

1. What couldn't Kirk understand?
   a. the plan b. the menu c. the weather forecast
2. At dinner, Ellen was distracted by her:
   a. communicator b. nails c. hair
3. Luke thought he knew _____ pretty well?
   a. phonics b. physics c. math
4. A phoneme is a:
   a. unit of sound b. word c. singing group
5. The English children went to _____ to stop the karaoke contest?
   a. Phonics City b. Mars c. the kitchen

Step 2 Solutions

1. **To whom did Bo belong?** Ben
2. **What pet did Bo not like?** cats
3. **Where did Ben and Bo live?** farm
4. **Why did Bo keep running after the cat at the top of the barn?** He could not stop.
5. **Why didn't Bo chase cats at the end of the story?** He hit hard.

Step 3 Solutions

2. What time of day do howler monkeys howl? 2
3. The more monkeys there are, the more they what? 4
4. One reason males howl is? 3
5. How far can the sound of a howling monkey travel? 5

OFFICIAL GUARDIAN MAIL

Mission 4: Identifying Fiction & Nonfiction

Attention trusted guardians:

We are in the midst of a very dangerous time. You may have noticed strange things happening. The Gremlin has marked all fiction books as nonfiction in our library catalog. That means that fiction books are being thought of as true stories. They are coming to life!

We need your help to change fiction books back to nonfiction before some scary things start happening! Thank you in advance for doing what you can as soon as possible.

Sincerely,

Kirk, Luke, and Ellen English

Guardians of Grammar Galaxy

☆ Step 1: Stay On Guard & Determine Fiction or Nonfiction by Subject Area

On Guard. *Highlight TRUE or FALSE for each statement.*

1. If you can't understand what you read, you have poor reading comprehension. TRUE FALSE
2. One way to understand what you read better is to put away electronics. TRUE FALSE
3. A homograph is a word that writes itself. TRUE FALSE
4. Clue words can help you decide what a homograph means. TRUE FALSE
5. Pictures can help you decide what a homograph means. TRUE FALSE

Say each of these words in a sentence. *Their meanings are given.*

regal – *royal* **mystified** – *confused* **fitfully** – *poorly*

Determine fiction or nonfiction by type of book. *Remember when you were asked about your interests to see what kinds of books you might like in Mission 1? This time, circle ALL THE FICTION SUBJECTS from the pictures on this page. Some subjects could be both fiction and nonfiction. Circle it if is mostly fiction.* ***Hint:*** *Stories are fiction.*

science fiction

graphic novels

historical stories

fairy tales

real-life stories

modern fantasy

places

jobs

animals

people

history

science

sports

☆ Step 2: Determine Fiction or Nonfiction by Content and Title

Highlight fiction or nonfiction for each book description.

1.	A book about how to take care of your dog.	FICTION NONFICTION
2.	A book about a cat who is a super hero.	FICTION NONFICTION
3.	A book about the sport of soccer.	FICTION NONFICTION
4.	A book about the life of President Abraham Lincoln.	FICTION NONFICTION
5.	A book about how the *Star Wars* movies were made.	FICTION NONFICTION

Activity. *Sort 10 books you have at home into piles of fiction and nonfiction. Be sure to put them back when you are done.*

☆ Step 3: Determine Fiction or Nonfiction for Sentences

Determine whether sentences are from fiction or nonfiction books.
Highlight FICTION or NONFICTION for each sentence.

1. Make sure you have the right food for your new puppy.	FICTION NONFICTION
2. Jones the cat put on his cape and flew out the window.	FICTION NONFICTION
3. Soccer is the most popular sport in the world.	FICTION NONFICTION
4. Abraham Lincoln was our 16th president.	FICTION NONFICTION
5. The first *Star Wars* movie was released in 1977.	FICTION NONFICTION

Vocabulary Victory! *Do you remember what these words mean? Check Step 1 if you forgot.*

regal **mystified** **fitfully**

☆ Advanced Guardians Only

Write or dictate (say) a sentence about which fiction book you would like to be nonfiction and why.

OFFICIAL GUARDIAN MAIL

Mission 4: Update

Dear guardians,

We are so proud to report that you have changed the category of a great number of books from nonfiction back to fiction. We have much less to worry about now!

But please be aware that there are some titles that haven't been labeled correctly. We will call on you to assign them to fiction or nonfiction in future missions, even though Luke is wanting some of his favorite fiction books to come to life.

We are sure you did your mission correctly, but just in case, we are sending you the solutions.

Sincerely,

Kirk, Luke, and Ellen English

Guardians of Grammar Galaxy

P.S. Are you filling in your reading calendar?

Step 1 Solutions

On Guard.

1. If you can't understand what you read, you have poor reading comprehension. **TRUE** FALSE
2. One way to understand what you read better is to put away electronics. **TRUE** FALSE
3. A homograph is a word that writes itself. TRUE **FALSE**
4. Clue words can help you decide what a homograph means. **TRUE** FALSE
5. Pictures can help you decide what a homograph means. **TRUE** FALSE

Determine Fiction or Nonfiction by Type of Book

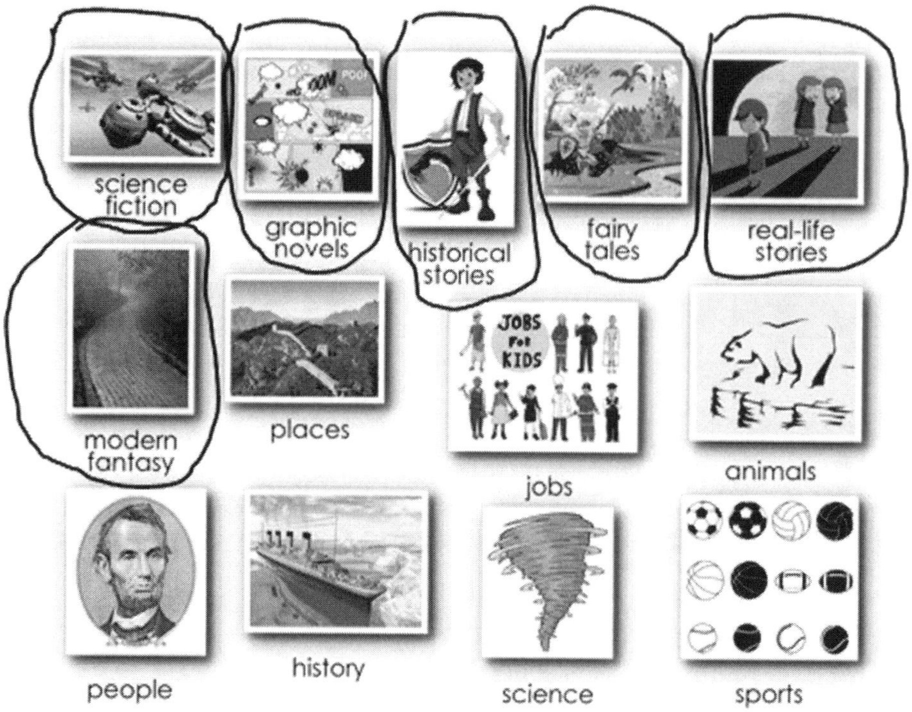

Step 2 Solutions

1. A book about how to take care of your dog. FICTION NONFICTION
2. A book about a cat who is a super hero. FICTION NONFICTION
3. A book about the sport of soccer. FICTION NONFICTION
4. A book about the life of President Abraham Lincoln. FICTION NONFICTION
5. A book about how the *Star Wars* movies were made. FICTION NONFICTION

Step 3 Solutions

1. Make sure you have the right food for your new puppy. FICTION NONFICTION
2. Jones the cat put on his cape and flew out the window. FICTION NONFICTION
3. Soccer is the most popular sport in the world. FICTION NONFICTION
4. Abraham Lincoln was our 16th president. FICTION NONFICTION
5. The first *Star Wars* movie was released in 1977. FICTION NONFICTION

OFFICIAL GUARDIAN MAIL

Mission 5: Story Elements

Attention galaxy guardians:

We have a crisis much like the fiction and nonfiction one we had. This time the characters, settings, and plots of books have gotten all mixed up! Please help us sort them out or literature won't be fun to read anymore.

We know you can do it!

Sincerely,

Kirk, Luke, and Ellen English

Guardians of Grammar Galaxy

☆ Step 1: On Guard & Matching Characters to Setting

On Guard. *Answer the following five questions for your teacher verbally (out loud).*

1. What is the difference between a fiction and a nonfiction book?

2. What is reading comprehension?

3. What is a homograph?

4. Name two ways to know the meaning of a homograph.

5. What are two kinds of books you like to read?

Say each of these words in a sentence. *Their meanings are given.*

graciously – *politely* **sequel** – *part two* **corrupted** – *damaged*

Match characters to setting. *Draw a line from the character to its most likely setting.*

☆ Step 2: Identify Character, Setting, and Plot

For the following, highlight whether it's a character, setting, or plot.

1. A gorilla

   CHARACTER SETTING PLOT

2. Gets into the zookeeper's bed

   CHARACTER SETTING PLOT

3. Zoo

   CHARACTER SETTING PLOT

4. Zookeeper

   CHARACTER SETTING PLOT

5. Zookeeper's house

   CHARACTER SETTING PLOT

Activity. *Go back to your list of three favorite books from Mission 1 and tell your teacher about the characters, setting, and plot for each.*

☆Step 3: Determining Characters, Setting, and Plot from Popular Literature

Highlight character, plot, or context for each question.

1. In the book *The Cat in the Hat* the cat is a:
   CHARACTER SETTING PLOT

2. In the story of *Little Red Riding Hood*, the forest is the:
   CHARACTER SETTING PLOT

3. In the story of *Cinderella*, losing her glass slipper at the ball is:
   CHARACTER SETTING PLOT

4. In the story of *The Little Red Hen*, getting no help making bread is:
   CHARACTER SETTING PLOT

5. In the story of *The Little Engine That Could*, the train is a:
   CHARACTER SETTING PLOT

Vocabulary Victory! *Do you remember what these words mean? Check Step 1 if you forgot.*

graciously **sequel** **corrupted**

☆ Advanced Guardians Only

Mix up the characters, setting, and plots of your favorite books to make a funny sentence. *Write or dictate it.*

The book ______________________________

is about the character(s) ______________________________

who live(s) in ______________________________ and

they ______________________________.

OFFICIAL GUARDIAN MAIL

Mission 5: Update

Dear guardian friends,

Thank you so much for doing your part to sort the characters, settings, and plots of books in the galaxy. We think we have fixed most of the books, but we may need your help again. You all are characters in a story that seems to have a plot with a happy ending!

Just in case, we are attaching the solutions to the problems we sent you.

Sincerely,

Kirk, Luke, and Ellen English

Guardians of Grammar Galaxy

Step 1 Solutions

On Guard.

1. **What is the difference between a fiction and a nonfiction book?** A fiction book isn't true like a fairy tale, while a nonfiction book is true.
2. **What is reading comprehension?** Reading comprehension is understanding what you read.
3. **What is a homograph?** A homograph is a word that can have more than one meaning even though it's spelled the same.
4. **Name two ways to know the meaning of a homograph.** Pictures and other words in a sentence can give you the meaning of a homograph.

Match Characters to Setting

Step 2 Solutions

1. **A gorilla**
   CHARACTER SETTING PLOT
2. **Gets into the zookeeper's bed**
   CHARACTER SETTING PLOT
3. **Zoo**
   CHARACTER SETTING PLOT
4. **Zookeeper**
   CHARACTER SETTING PLOT
5. **Zookeeper's house**
   CHARACTER SETTING PLOT

Step 3 Solutions

1. In the book, *The Cat in the Hat*, the cat is a:
   CHARACTER SETTING PLOT
2. In the story of *Little Red Riding Hood*, the forest is the:
   CHARACTER SETTING PLOT
3. In the story of *Cinderella*, losing her glass slipper at the ball is:
   CHARACTER SETTING PLOT
4. In the story of the *Little Red Hen*, getting no help making bread is:
   CHARACTER SETTING PLOT
5. In the story of *The Little Engine That Could*, the train is a:
   CHARACTER SETTING PLOT

OFFICIAL GUARDIAN MAIL

Mission 6: Tall Tales

Dear guardian friends,

We are writing to you today about our father's biography. No doubt you have been looking forward to reading it, but we are afraid there is a problem with it. It isn't entirely truthful. In fact, it's more of a tall tale than a biography. And that's why we need your help. Because the book is listed as nonfiction, everything that is written in it is coming true. Remember the last time that happened?

We need you to learn to identify tall tales and the parts of our father's biography that are unbelievable, so we can ask the writer to change them. We hope our father will become his old self once again.

We are counting on you!

Sincerely,

Kirk, Luke, and Ellen English

Guardians of Grammar Galaxy

☆ Step 1: On Guard & Identify Tall Tales from Pictures

On Guard. *Highlight a, b, or c as the best answer.*

1. A setting is:
   a. the person the story is about
   b. what happens in the story
   c. where and when the story happens

2. A book that has characters, a setting, and a plot is most likely:
   a. fiction
   b. nonfiction
   c. neither fiction or nonfiction

3. Reading comprehension will be poor if:
   a. a student can't see well
   b. a student doesn't know phonics
   c. both a and b

4. Which of the following is a homograph:
   a. the
   b. can
   c. spaceship

5. Which homograph belongs in the blanks? The dog started to _____ when the squirrel jumped onto the _____ of the tree.
   a. wave
   b. down
   c. bark

Say each of these words in a sentence. *Their meanings are given.*

triumphantly – *victoriously* **shadowing** – *following* **elated** – *thrilled*

Circle the pictures that would be part of a tall tale.

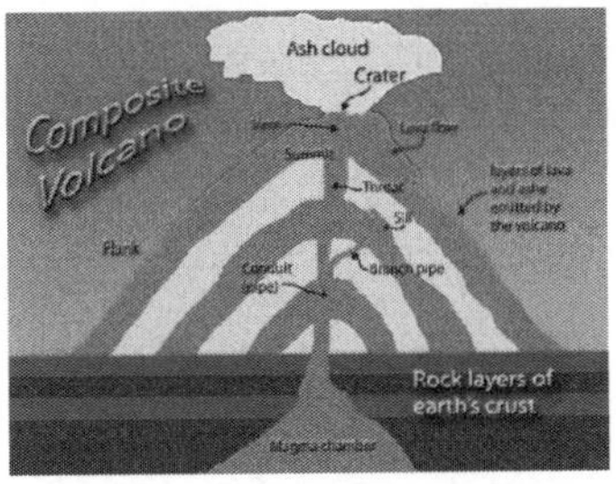

☆ Step 2: Identify & Tell Tall Tales

Identify parts of the king's biography that are exaggerated or unbelievable. *Which of the following statements from the book make it a tall tale? Highlight the number in front of the unbelievable sentences.*

1. The king of Grammar Galaxy is so strong he has stopped meteors from crashing into planet English with his bare hands.

2. The king of Grammar Galaxy is fond of eggs for breakfast.

3. The king of Grammar Galaxy has memorized the entire dictionary.

4. The king of Grammar Galaxy has given away more gold than has been mined in the last thousand years.

5. The king of Grammar Galaxy is a handsome man.

Activity. *Tell your teacher, siblings, or friends three tall tales—one of which is actually true, but sounds like a tall tale. See if they can guess which tale is true.*

☆ Step 3: Identify Other Tall Tale Biographies

For each sentence that is part of a tall tale, explain to your teacher why it is unbelievable.

1. Johnny Appleseed planted all the apple trees in the West.

2. Pecos Bill used snakes as lassos and whips.

3. Paul Bunyan could eat 50 pancakes in one minute.

4. Calamity Jane swam 90 miles of the Platte River at top speed.

5. Sometimes you can still hear John Henry's two hammers that built the railroad in the 1800s.

Vocabulary Victory! *Do you remember what these words mean? Check Step 1 if you forgot.*

triumphantly **shadowing** **elated**

☆ Advanced Guardians Only

Read a tall tale about one of the American legends underlined in Step 3. *You will find some titles at http://GrammarGalaxyBooks.com/Nebula.*

OFFICIAL GUARDIAN MAIL

Mission 6: Update

Dear guardian friends,

Thank you for helping to identify tall tales. As a result of your hard work, we have been able to convince the king that his biography needs to be rewritten. He is disappointed, but we are relieved that he is seeming more like himself.

We hope you will be on the lookout for more tall tales labeled as nonfiction. Here are the solutions to your mission. We don't think it's an exaggeration to say that you're amazing!

Sincerely,

Kirk, Luke, and Ellen English

Guardians of Grammar Galaxy

Step 1 Solutions

On Guard.

1. A setting is:
   - a. The person the story is about
   - b. What happens in the story
   - c. Where and when the story happens
2. A book that has characters, a setting, and a plot is most likely:
   - a. Fiction
   - b. Nonfiction
   - c. Neither fiction or nonfiction
3. Reading comprehension will be poor if:
   - a. A student can't see well
   - b. A student doesn't know phonics
   - c. Both a and b
4. Which of the following is a homograph:
   - a. The
   - b. Can
   - c. Spaceship
5. Which homograph belongs in the blanks? The dog started to _____ when the squirrel jumped onto the _____ of the tree.

a. wave
b. down
c. bark

Identify Tall Tales from Pictures

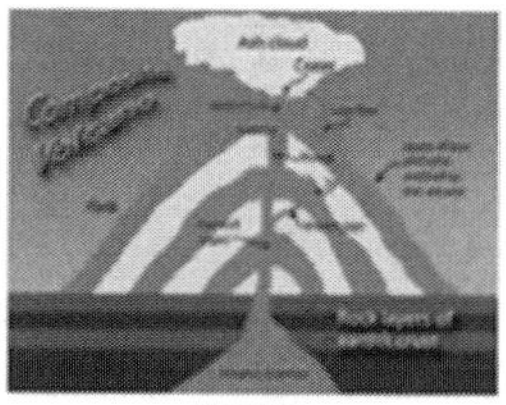

Step 2 Solutions

1. The king of Grammar Galaxy is so strong, he has stopped meteors from crashing into planet English with his bare hands.
2. The king of Grammar Galaxy is fond of eggs for breakfast.
3. The king of Grammar Galaxy has memorized the entire dictionary.
4. The king of Grammar Galaxy has given away more gold than has been mined in the last thousand years.
5. The king of Grammar Galaxy is a handsome man.

Step 3 Solutions: *Answers may vary.*

1. **Johnny Appleseed** planted all the apple trees in the West.
   One man couldn't have planted all the apple trees in the West.
2. **Pecos Bill** used snakes as lassos and whips.
   Snakes can't be tied tightly like lassos and wouldn't work as whips. Venomous snakes are also too dangerous.
3. **Paul Bunyan** could eat 50 pancakes in one minute.
   A giant could eat 50 pancakes in a minute, but there has never been a man big enough to do that.
4. **Calamity Jane** swam 90 miles of the Platte River at top speed.
   Swimming 90 miles would be difficult but impossible at top speed.
5. Sometimes you can still hear **John Henry**'s two hammers that built the railroad in the 1800s.
   Sounds don't last for two hundred years.

OFFICIAL GUARDIAN MAIL

Mission 7: Rhyming Words

Dear fellow guardians,

We have another serious problem—this time in Poetry City. A company called Word Harmony is matching words that don't rhyme. The result is terrible for our rhyming poems and books.

We need your help to match the rhyming words that truly belong together. We know you can do it so great books like *Green Eggs and Ham* can be enjoyed once again.

Sincerely,

Kirk, Luke, and Ellen English

Guardians of Grammar Galaxy

☆ Step 1: On Guard & Match Rhyming Pictures

On Guard. *Highlight TRUE or FALSE for each statement.*

1. Words that rhyme end with the same sound. TRUE FALSE

2. A tall tale can also be called a folk tale. TRUE FALSE

3. Reading for fun can't help you get better grades. TRUE FALSE

4. Other words in a sentence can be clues to the meaning of a word you don't know. TRUE FALSE

5. A tall tale may be written like a biography that is too unbelievable to be true. TRUE FALSE

Say each of these words in a sentence. *Their meanings are given.*

indignantly – *angrily* **sullenly** – *pouting* **aghast** – *shocked*

Match rhyming pictures. *Draw a line between pictures of objects with names that rhyme.*

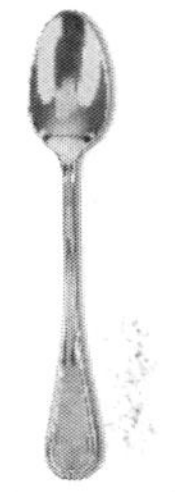

☆ Step 2: Identify Rhyming Words by Ending Sounds

Do the following words that have been matched in Poetry City belong together because they rhyme? *Highlight YES or NO for each.*

1. lip & dip YES NO
2. den & rim YES NO
3. or & for YES NO
4. pet & tip YES NO
5. land & stand YES NO

Activity. *See how many words you can say that rhyme with* ***at*** *in 30 seconds.* ***Hint:*** *Use the alphabet to come up with more words.*

☆ Step 3: Complete a Rhyming Poem

Add the missing letters so the word rhymes with the last word in the line above and the poem makes sense.

My sister went to the **zoo**.

I got to go along __oo.

We packed some drinks and some **grapes**.

I wanted to see the __pes.

But soon it started to **rain**.

So we could not ride the __rain.

We found all the apes **inside**

Where they did not try to __ide.

We had fun, though we got **wet**.

I took an ape home as a __et.

Is this poem a tall tale?

Hint: *You'll use the letters t, a, h, and p in the blanks.*

Vocabulary Victory! *Do you remember what these words mean? Check Step 1 if you forgot.*

indignantly **sullenly** **aghast**

☆ Advanced Guardians Only

Write or dictate your own rhyme. *Make sure the last word in each line ends with the same sound.*

OFFICIAL GUARDIAN MAIL

Mission 7: Update

Dear guardian friends,

We are pleased to report that we have had success in putting the right words together in rhyming pairs. And as of now, Word Harmony is out of business.

Thank you so much for all your help. You are excellent matchmakers! We are enclosing not only the solutions to the matches we asked you to make, but also restored lines of poetry for you to enjoy.

Sincerely,

Kirk, Luke, and Ellen English

Guardians of Grammar Galaxy

P.S. We almost forgot! You have completed all the missions required to earn your star for literature. We just need to make sure you are ready to defend the galaxy against any future attacks on our stories and poems. We are attaching the Literature Challenge. Your teacher can read it to you. If you get 9 out of 10 questions correct, you will earn your star! If you don't pass the challenge the first time, review the correct answers and try again. We know you can do it!

Corrected Poetry from the Story

I think that I shall never see
A poem as lovely as a tree.

I'm number one; can't be number two.
I just called a checkmate on you.

Do you like green eggs and ham?
I do not like them, Sam-I-Am.

I do not like green eggs and ham!

Then our mother came in
And she said to us two,
"Did you have any fun?
Tell me. What did you do?"

Step 1 Solutions

On Guard.

1. Words that rhyme end with the same sound. TRUE FALSE
2. A tall tale can also be called a folk tale. TRUE FALSE
3. Reading for fun can't help you get better grades. TRUE FALSE
4. Other words in a sentence can be clues to the meaning of a word you don't know. TRUE FALSE
5. A tall tale may be written like a biography that is too unbelievable to be true. TRUE FALSE

Step 2 Solutions

1. lip & dip YES NO
2. den & rim YES NO

3. or & for — YES NO

4. pet & tip — YES NO

5. land & stand — YES NO

Step 3 Solutions

My sister went to the zoo.
I got to go along too.
We packed some drinks and some grapes.
I wanted to see the apes.
But soon it started to rain.
So we could not ride the train.
We found all the apes inside
Where they did not try to hide.
We had fun, though we got wet.
I took an ape home as a pet.

Is this poem a tall tale? Yes.

Literature Challenge I

Carefully read or listen to all the possible answers *and then highlight the letter for the* ***one*** ***best answer****.*

1. **A homograph is:**
   a. A word that is spelled the same as another word, but has a different meaning
   b. A word that is spelled differently from another word, but has the same meaning
   c. A word that rhymes with another word
2. **To determine the meaning of a word in a sentence:**
   a. Look for clues in any pictures
   b. Look at the other words in the sentence
   c. Look for clues in any pictures and in other words in the sentence
3. **Understanding what we read is called:**
   a. Story elements
   b. Tall tales
   c. Reading comprehension
4. **Reading comprehension can be poor because of:**
   a. Poor vision or hearing
   b. Being distracted
   c. Poor vision or hearing, being distracted, or poor phonics skills
5. **The following book is an example of fiction:**
   a. *The Cat in the Hat*
   b. *The History of Hats*
   c. *All About Cats*
6. **The following book is an example of nonfiction:**
   a. *The Dinosaur Who Lived in My Backyard*
   b. *All About Dinosaurs*
   c. *How Do Dinosaurs Say Good-night?*

7. The setting of a book is:

a. When and where a story takes place

b. Where you can find it in the library

c. Where you keep it at home

8. The following is an example of a plot:

a. The three little pigs

b. The wolf

c. The wolf trying to blow the three little pigs' houses down

9. A tall tale is also called:

a. A long tale

b. A fish story

c. A ladder story

10. Words that rhyme:

a. Are often found in poems

b. End in the same sounds

c. End in the same sounds and are often found in poems

Number Correct:________/10

☆ Extra Challenge

How many of these vocabulary words can you remember the meaning of?

indignantly	**sullenly**	**aghast**	**triumphantly**
shadowing	**elated**	**graciously**	**sequel**
corrupted	**regal**	**mystified**	**fitfully**
dilemma	**phonemes**	**astounded**	**ecstatic**
fibbing	**excursion**	**exquisite**	**inestimable**
tenacity	**composition**		

Number Correct:________/22

Literature Challenge 1 Answers

1.a; 2.c; 3.c; 4.c; 5.a; 6.b; 7.a; 8.c; 9.b; 10.c

If you got 9 or more correct, congratulations! You've earned your Literature Star. You can color the star or add a sticker to your Grammar Guardian bookmark. You can print a bookmark on cardstock with your teacher's help from the printables at http://GrammarGalaxyBooks.com/Nebula. You are ready for an adventure in vocabulary.

If you did not get 9 or more correct, don't worry. You have another chance. You may want to have your teacher review the information in the guidebook for each story you've read so far. Then take the Literature Challenge 2. Remember to **choose the one best answer**.

Extra Challenge Answers

Here are the meanings of the vocabulary words. Review, say them in a sentence, and see if you can remember more of them.

indignantly - *angrily*
triumphantly - *victoriously*
graciously - *politely*
regal - *royal*
dilemma - *problem*
ecstatic - *thrilled*
exquisite - *beautiful*
composition - *writing*
sullenly - *pouting*
shadowing - *following*
sequel - *part two*
mystified - *confused*
phonemes – units of sound
fibbing - *lying*
inestimable - *valuable*
aghast - *shocked*
elated - *thrilled*
corrupted - *damaged*
fitfully - *poorly*
astounded - *shocked*
excursion – *trip*
tenacity – *determination*

Literature Challenge 2

***Carefully read or listen to all the possible answers** and then highlight the letter for the __one__ **best answer**.*

1. **Words that are spelled the same as another word but have a different meaning are called:**
   a. Hieroglyphics
   b. Homographs
   c. Twin words
2. **Pictures and other words in a sentence can be clues to:**
   a. The order of the alphabet
   b. Who ate the last of the ice cream at your house
   c. The meaning of a homograph or any missing word in a sentence
3. **Reading comprehension is:**
   a. A story element
   b. A tall tale
   c. Understanding what is read
4. **Poor phonics skills can cause:**
   a. Poor reading comprehension
   b. Fiction stories to come to life
   c. Homographs to lose their meaning
5. ***Little Red Riding Hood* is an example of:**
   a. A fairy tale
   b. Fiction
   c. Both a fairy tale and fiction
6. ***The World's Biggest Volcanoes* is an example of:**
   a. A nonfiction book
   b. A tall tale
   c. A fiction book

7. **Little Red Riding Hood is an example of:**
   a. A setting
   b. A character
   c. A plot
8. **The wolf pretending to be Little Red Riding Hood's granny is an example of:**
   a. A plot
   b. A character
   c. A setting
9. **Books about Paul Bunyan:**
   a. Are folk tales
   b. Are fiction
   c. Are folk tales, fiction, and tall tales
10. **Pan and man are examples of words that:**
    a. Rhyme
    b. Are homographs
    c. Rhyme and are homographs

Number Correct:________/10

Literature Challenge 2 Answers

1.b; 2.c; 3.c; 4.a; 5.c; 6.a; 7.b; 8.a; 9.c; 10.a

If you got 9 or more correct, congratulations! You've earned your Literature Star. You can color the star or add a sticker to your Grammar Guardian bookmark. You can print a bookmark on cardstock with your teacher's help from the printables at http://GrammarGalaxyBooks.com/Nebula. You are ready for an adventure in vocabulary.

If you did not get 9 or more correct, don't worry. Review the questions you missed with your teacher. You may want to get more practice using the resources at http://GalaxyGrammarBooks.com/Nebula. Your teacher can ask you other questions like the ones you missed and if you get them correct, you'll have earned your Literature Star and can move on to an adventure in vocabulary.

Unit II: Adventures in Vocabulary

OFFICIAL GUARDIAN MAIL

Mission 8: Synonyms and Antonyms

Attention guardians:

A policy change by the Thesaurus Office in Synonym City has created a crisis. No doubt you've already noticed that you are often saying the opposite of what you mean! Ellen has already suffered an injury as a result. We want to prevent any more harm from being done, but we need your help.

Identify the synonyms (words with similar meanings) that belong together as well as the antonyms (words with opposite meanings) that don't belong with them.

Thank you in advance! We will give you an update on Ellen when your mission is complete.

Sincerely,

Kirk and Luke English

Guardians of Grammar Galaxy

☆ Step 1: On Guard & Match Antonyms in Pictures

On Guard. *Highlight TRUE or FALSE for each statement.*

1. Synonyms are words that end with the same sound. TRUE FALSE
2. Antonyms are words that have opposite meaning. TRUE FALSE
3. You find rhyming words in a thesaurus. TRUE FALSE
4. Other words and pictures are the context of a sentence. TRUE FALSE
5. Only nonfiction books can make you smarter. TRUE FALSE

Say each of these words in a sentence. *Their meanings are given.*

engrossed – *occupied* **infirmary** – *hospital* **diversity** – *variety*

Match antonyms in pictures. *Draw a line between pictures of objects that have opposite meaning.*

☆ Step 2: Identify Synonyms and Antonyms

The following words are living together in Synonym City. But are they synonyms or antonyms? *Highlight SYNONYM or ANTONYM for each word pair.*

1. thin & slim SYNONYM ANTONYM
2. sick & ill SYNONYM ANTONYM
3. sad & glad SYNONYM ANTONYM
4. mom & mother SYNONYM ANTONYM
5. down & up SYNONYM ANTONYM

Activity. *Try using antonyms (saying the opposite of what you mean) at your next meal and see how much trouble it causes for antonyms to get mixed up with synonyms.* ***Hint:*** *Make sure your family knows what you are doing!*

☆ Step 3: Help the Thesaurus Office Match Synonyms

The following words in Synonym City want roommates. *Tell your teacher which words are synonyms and should live with them and which words are antonyms and should not. When you can't think of any more, have your teacher help you use a thesaurus or thesaurus.com to find more.*

1. Pretty	SYNONYMS?	ANTONYMS?
2. Good	SYNONYMS?	ANTONYMS?
3. Tasty	SYNONYMS?	ANTONYMS?
4. Cold	SYNONYMS?	ANTONYMS?
5. Quick	SYNONYMS?	ANTONYMS?

Vocabulary Victory! *Do you remember what these words mean? Check Step 1 if you forgot.*

engrossed **infirmary** **diversity**

☆ Advanced Guardians Only

Rewrite or dictate this sentence using synonyms for the underlined words. Use a thesaurus if you like. *The kid had a good time with good friends.* ***Hint:*** *You may have to change the* **a** *before good to* **an** *if your synonym starts with a vowel sound.*

OFFICIAL GUARDIAN MAIL

Mission 8: Update

Dear guardians,

We are so happy to tell you that Ellen is doing much better. And the really good news is that we have helped to move many antonyms out of Synonym City. The result is that we aren't saying the opposite of what we mean.

Unfortunately, there are a few antonyms that we missed. In future missions, we'll be asking you to find them in the On Guard section. Thank you in advance for your service to the galaxy.

As usual, we are attaching the solutions to this mission.

Sincerely,

Kirk and Luke English

Guardians of Grammar Galaxy

<u>Step 1 Solutions</u>

On Guard.

1. Synonyms are words that end with the same sound. TRUE **FALSE**
2. Antonyms are words that have opposite meaning. **TRUE** FALSE
3. You find rhyming words in a thesaurus. TRUE **FALSE**
4. Other words and pictures are the context of a sentence. **TRUE** FALSE
5. Only nonfiction books can make you smarter. TRUE **FALSE**

Match antonyms in pictures

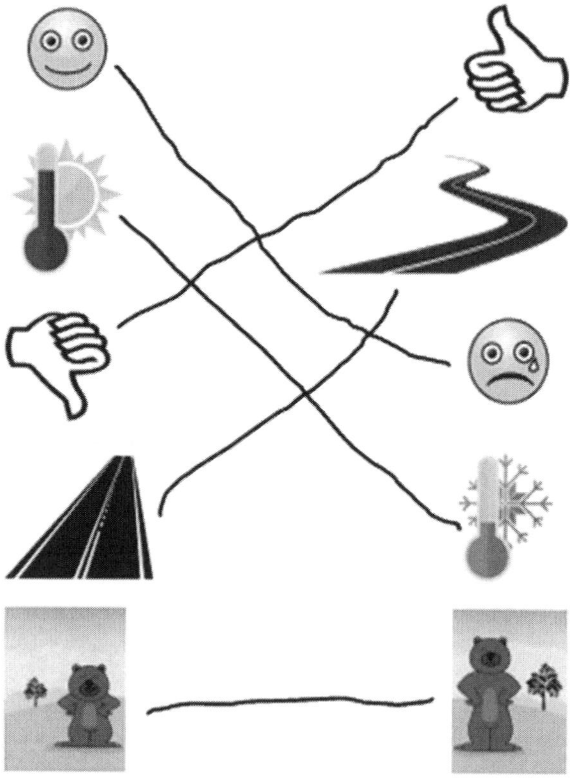

Step 2 Solutions

1. thin	&	slim	SYNONYM	ANTONYM
2. sick	&	ill	SYNONYM	ANTONYM
3. sad	&	glad	SYNONYM	ANTONYM
4. mom	&	mother	SYNONYM	ANTONYM
5. down	&	up	SYNONYM	ANTONYM

Step 3 Solutions: *Answers may vary*

1. Pretty SYNONYMS: attractive, beautiful, lovely, nice-looking, appealing; ANTONYMS: ugly, unpleasant, horrible, dreadful, horrid
2. Good SYNONYMS: fine, great, excellent, nice, lovely, satisfactory, enjoyable; ANTONYMS: bad, poor, harmful, awful
3. Tasty SYNONYMS: yummy, delicious, scrumptious, appetizing, mouthwatering; ANTONYMS: tasteless, yucky, icky, disgusting
4. Cold SYNONYMS: icy, cool, freezing, frigid, frosty; ANTONYMS: warm, hot, toasty, steamy, burning
5. Quick SYNONYMS: fast, speedy, rapid, hasty, hurried; ANTONYMS: slow, gradual, dawdling, relaxed, unhurried

OFFICIAL GUARDIAN MAIL

Mission 9: Vocabulary

Dear trusted guardians,

We are sure you remember the crisis we faced when we weren't reading. One of the things that happened was the weakening and even disappearance of words from planet Vocabulary. When we don't use words often enough, their accounts on Wordbook are being closed. We are hoping the king can stop Wordbook from doing this, but in the meantime, we need your help.

First, we need you to read. The more you read, the more your vocabulary will increase. **Second, we need you to learn the meaning of new words**. Every time you see or hear a word you don't know, we need you to do one of three things: 1) ask for the meaning of the word; 2) look up the meaning of a word in a digital book (usually by tapping and holding the word); or 3) use an adhesive flag to mark the page and the unknown word in a printed book. Instead of interrupting your reading, flag the word and ask the meaning or look it up later in a digital or printed dictionary with your teacher's help. **Third, we want you to create your own word book**. Add the words you didn't know and their definitions (meanings). Include a synonym or picture (draw or print it) to help you remember what it means. We are including pages you can use to create your own word book or your teacher can print them off at http://GrammarGalaxyBooks.com/Nebula. **Finally, please complete the following mission** which will increase your vocabulary and will save more words.

Sincerely,

Kirk, Luke, and Ellen English

Guardians of Grammar Galaxy

☆ Step 1: On Guard & Choose New Vocabulary Words

On Guard. *Highlight the correct answer for each statement.*

1. First and second graders should be learning about:
   2,000 new words a day   2 new words a day

2. Synonyms are words that mean the:
   same   opposite

3. Which of the following word pairs are homographs?
   big large   wind wind

4. Which of the following words rhyme with log?
   dog   bag

5. A biography is:
   always a tall tale   a book about someone's life

Say each of these words in a sentence. *Their meanings are given.*

mortified – *ashamed*   **grousing** – *complaining*   **appease** – *please*

Choose new vocabulary words. *Highlight the synonyms below that you have not read or heard before. There are no right or wrong answers.*

1. **Good**: noble, beneficial, superior, proficient
2. **Went**: left, traveled, proceeded, departed
3. **Said**: spoke, uttered, declared, articulated
4. **Thought**: believed, considered, reflected, pondered
5. **Got**: found, obtained, procured, acquired

☆ Step 2: Use New Vocabulary

Learn the meaning of new vocabulary words. *Highlight the word that is a synonym for each word after reading its meaning.*

1. **Witticism**: a clever or funny remark

   joke   cartoon   balloon

2. **Emulate**: to try to be like

   ignore   copy   necklace

3. **Applaud**: express approval, especially by putting hands together

   eat   put   clap

4. **Narrative**: a tale, as in a fairy tale

   story   fishing   shaving

5. **Pivot**: the action of turning around a point

   duck   spin   scoot

Activity. *Don't look at your mission manual and have your teacher give you the following commands. Can you follow them?*

1. Emulate a dog.
2. Give me a narrative of a dog.
3. Tell me a witticism.
4. Applaud yourself.
5. Pivot as quickly as you can.

☆ Step 3: Review Vocabulary Words

Review the three vocabulary words from Step 1. *Then demonstrate for your teacher how you would react to the command to clean your room if you were:*

1. mortified

2. grousing

3. wanting to appease your parent

Use Your Word Book. *With your teacher's help, create your own word book with the pages that follow. Your teacher may want to three-hole punch the pages and put them into a binder or bind them in another way. Color the front cover or print a colored cover from http://GrammarGalaxyBooks.com/Nebula. Have your teacher print more pages from the website or copy them from the book.* Then complete these steps for each new word you find:

1. Date the top of each page. You'll be able to track how many new words you are learning! **Note:** Some words you will learn without reading them, so they won't be in your book. That's OK!
2. Write a word you don't know on the handwriting lines.
3. Get help looking up the word in a dictionary.
4. Print out or draw a picture to help you remember the word's meaning if you can (some words can't be drawn easily).
5. Ask your teacher to write or help you print and paste a synonym and definition for the word. **Note**: The word *definition* is the same as the meaning.

My
Word
Book

Words Learned Since ___________

New Word ______________________

Synonym:

Definition:

New Word ______________________

Synonym:

Definition:

New Word ______________________

Synonym:

Definition:

New Word ______________________

Synonym:

Definition:

Vocabulary Victory! *Do you remember what these words mean? Check Step 1 if you forgot.*

mortified **grousing** **appease**

☆ Advanced Guardians Only

Write or dictate a sentence using one of the words in your word book.

OFFICIAL GUARDIAN MAIL

Mission 9: Update

Dear guardians,

Great news! You are learning so many new words that very few accounts on Wordbook are being closed. Please keep it up because we don't know how long it will take to change Wordbook's terms of service. Did you know that the more words you know, the more likely you are to make more money as an adult? And guess the easiest way to learn more words. You're right! It's reading!

Keep reading every day. Please make sure that you succeeded in this week's mission by checking the attached solutions with your teacher. Thanks again for your service to the galaxy!

Sincerely,

Kirk, Luke, and Ellen English

Guardians of Grammar Galaxy

Step 1 Solutions

On Guard.

1. First and second graders should be learning about:
   2,000 new words a day   2 new words a day
2. Synonyms are words that mean the:
   same   opposite
3. Which of the following word pairs are homographs:
   big large   wind wind
4. Which of the following words rhyme with log:
   dog   bag
5. A biography is:
   always a tall tale   a book about someone's life

Step 2 Solutions

1. **Witticism**: a clever or funny remark
   joke   cartoon   balloon
2. **Emulate**: to try to be like
   ignore   copy   necklace

3. **Applaud**: express approval, especially by putting hands together
   eat put clap
4. **Narrative**: a tale, as in a fairy tale
   story fishing shaving
5. **Pivot**: the action of turning around a point
   duck spin scoot

Step 3 Solutions:

1. mortified – look horrified or upset
2. grousing - complain
3. wanting to appease your parent – seem eager

OFFICIAL GUARDIAN MAIL

Mission 10: Fix the Prefixes

Dear galaxy guardians,

We are writing to inform you that two prefixes have created serious problems. They are **re-** and **un-**. They have changed the meaning of our words, but worst of all, the head programmer has managed to lock the king in the dungeon!

This is where you come in. Until we are able to completely remove these two viruses from the galaxy's computer system, we need you to fix these two prefixes. We believe we can get Father out of the dungeon and back on the throne if you succeed.

Thank you in advance for your help with this important mission!

Sincerely,

Kirk, Luke, and Ellen English

Guardians of Grammar Galaxy

☆ Step 1: On Guard & Choose the Correct Prefix

On Guard. *Answer the questions for your teacher.*

1. Why is reading so important?
2. What is the difference between fiction and nonfiction?
3. What is the setting of a story?
4. What is vocabulary?
5. What is a prefix?

Say each of these words in a sentence. *Their meanings are given.*

astonished – *surprised* **eerily** – *creepily* **replicating** – *copying*

Choose the correct prefix. *Draw a line from the* ***re-*** *or* ***un-*** *prefix to make a word.* ***Note:*** *<u>Some words may have lines drawn to both prefixes</u>. If you aren't sure if the prefix makes a word, ask your teacher to help you look it up in a dictionary.*

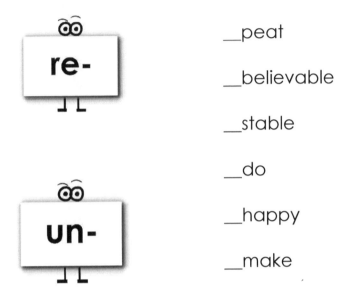

__peat

__believable

__stable

__do

__happy

__make

☆ Step 2: Choose Prefixes by Meaning

Read the meaning of the word. *Highlight the prefix that will give the root word that meaning.*

1. **Not kind**: __kind

   un- re-

2. **Think again**: __think

   un- re-

3. **Not fit**: __fit

   un- re-

4. **Open the zipper**: __zip

   un- re-

5. **Make new again**: __new

   un- re-

Activity. *Play Simon Says with your teacher using redo and undo. For example, your teacher may say, "Simon says take three bunny hops. Simon says redo." You would take three more bunny hops. If Simon says undo, you would take three bunny hops back.*

☆ Step 3: Use Prefixes in Context

Use the prefix that will help the king. *Highlight the prefix that will help the king and return the galaxy to normal.*

1. Un- Re- __tie the king.
2. Un- Re- __lock the king's cell.
3. Un- Re- __turn the king to the throne.
4. Un- Re- __move Prefix from the throne.
5. Un- Re- __do the viruses that caused problems.

Vocabulary Victory! *Do you remember what these words mean? Check Step 1 if you forgot.*

astonished **eerily** **replicating**

☆ Advanced Guardians Only

Write or dictate a sentence using a re- or un- word that would solve a problem Prefix has caused.

OFFICIAL GUARDIAN MAIL

Mission 10: Update

Dear great guardians,

You succeeded in returning Father to the throne! Prefix has also been removed from the castle. That's the good news. The bad news is we don't know where he is and we haven't been able to recapture the English language criminals who were released. We will have to be on the lookout for them and for **re-** and **un-** words. Add them to your word book if they are new to you. How many new words have you learned since last mission?

We are attaching the solutions to the prefix problems we sent you. Thanks again for your help! We are so happy things have **returned** to normal. That's a **re-** word we like!

Sincerely,

Kirk, Luke, and Ellen English

Guardians of Grammar Galaxy

Step 1 Solutions

On Guard.

1. **Why is reading so important?** Because future school and life success depends on it.
2. **What is the difference between fiction and nonfiction?** Fiction is made-up stories and nonfiction is factual.
3. **What is the setting of a story?** The place, time, and mood of a story.
4. **What is vocabulary?** The words that you know and use.
5. **What is a prefix?** The beginning part of a word that can be used to change its meaning.

Choose the correct prefix.

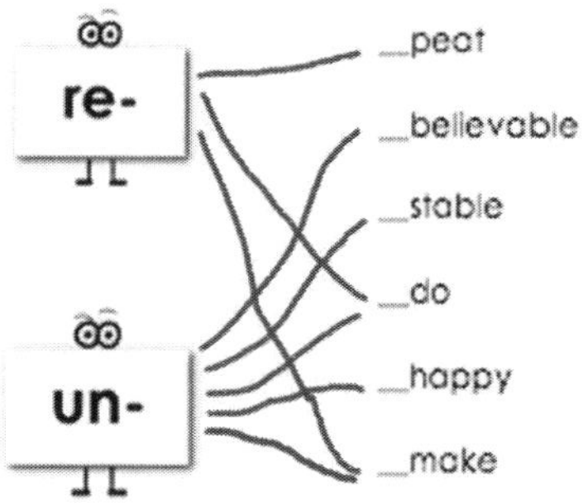

Step 2 Solutions

1. **Not kind**: __kind
   un- re-
2. **Think again**: __think
   un- re-
3. **Not fit**: __fit
   un- re-
4. **Open the zipper**: __zip
   un- re-
5. **Make new again**: __new
   un- re-

Step 3 Solutions

1. Un- Re- __tie the king.
2. Un- Re- __lock the king's cell.
3. Un- Re- __turn the king to the throne.
4. Un- Re- __move Prefix from the throne.
5. Un- Re- __do the viruses that caused problems.

OFFICIAL GUARDIAN MAIL

Mission 11: Fix the Suffixes

Dear friends,

We are afraid we have some bad news. Remember Prefix and all the problems he caused with **re-** and **un-**? Well, he is gone, but his twin brother Suffix is causing nearly as many problems.

Have the people who teach you disappeared? Are you unable to speak? Is everything lovely becoming ugly? Then you know what we are talking about. The suffixes **–er**, **–ful**, and **–less** aren't being used correctly. We are trying to find Suffix so we can fix them.

Until then, we need your help to get them sorted out. Thank you, faithful guardians!

Sincerely,

Kirk, Luke, and Ellen English

Guardians of Grammar Galaxy

☆ Step 1: On Guard & Choose the Correct Suffix

On Guard. *Highlight the correct answer.*

1. What is an antonym for hard?
   difficult tough soft

2. A word you know is part of your _____?
   toy box vocabulary homographs

3. Which prefix makes ___**view** a word?
   re- un-

4. *The Tale of Peter Rabbit* is an example of what?
   nonfiction fiction

5. In chapter 10, the word astonished means _____?
   frustrated surprised sad

Say each of these words in a sentence. *Their meanings are given.*

recounting – *describing* **tizzy** – *panic* **withering** – *dying*

Choose the correct suffix. *Draw a line from the* ***–er****,* ***–ful****, or* ***–less*** *suffix that makes a word that was messed up in chapter 11.*

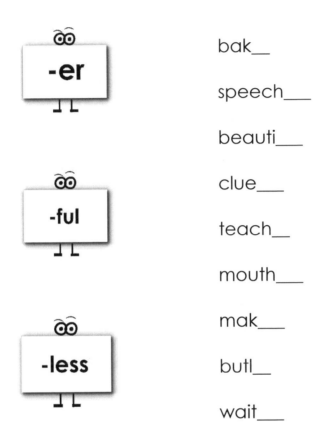

bak__

speech___

beauti___

clue___

teach__

mouth___

mak___

butl__

wait___

☆ Step 2: Choose Suffixes by Meaning

Read the meaning of the word. *Highlight the suffix that will give the root word that meaning.*

1. **Full of wonder**: wonder___

   -er -less -ful

2. **Someone who sends**: send___

   -er -less -ful

3. **Without power**: power___

   -er -less -ful

4. **Someone who takes**: tak___

   -er -less -ful

5. **Full of thanks**: thank___

   -er -less -ful

Activity. *Practice being speechless and communicate with your teacher without speaking for half an hour.*

☆ Step 3: Use Suffixes in Context

Highlight the positive suffixes. *Highlight the good words that were missing and causing problems for the English family.*

speechless	teacher	mouthful
butler	clueless	beautiful
maker	waiter	baker

Vocabulary Victory! *Do you remember what these words mean? Check Step 1 if you forgot.*

recounting	**tizzy**	**withering**

☆ Advanced Guardians Only

Complete the following sentence by writing or dictating to your teacher:

The most important suffix I learned is (highlight one) **–er –ful –less** because

OFFICIAL GUARDIAN MAIL

Mission 11: Update

Dear guardians,

We are excited to report these wonderful updates:

- Our teachers and staff have returned!
- We are no longer clueless and speechless.
- Our garden is beautiful once again.

We are hopeful that all is well where you are too. Thank you, thank you, thank you for all your help. We discovered that Suffix hacked our computer system and introduced another virus that caused all the problems. We are hopeful that we have fixed the suffixes!

Attached are the solutions to the mission you completed.

Sincerely,

Kirk, Luke, and Ellen English

Guardians of Grammar Galaxy

<u>Step 1 Solutions</u>

On Guard.

1. What is an antonym for <u>hard</u>?
   difficult   tough   soft
2. A word you know is part of your _____?
   toy box   vocabulary   homographs
3. Which prefix makes ___view a word?
   re-   un-
4. *The Tale of Peter Rabbit* is an example of what?
   nonfiction   fiction
5. In chapter 10, the word <u>astonished</u> means _____?
   frustrated   surprised   sad

Choose the Correct Suffix. *A line should be drawn from –er to all remaining words.*

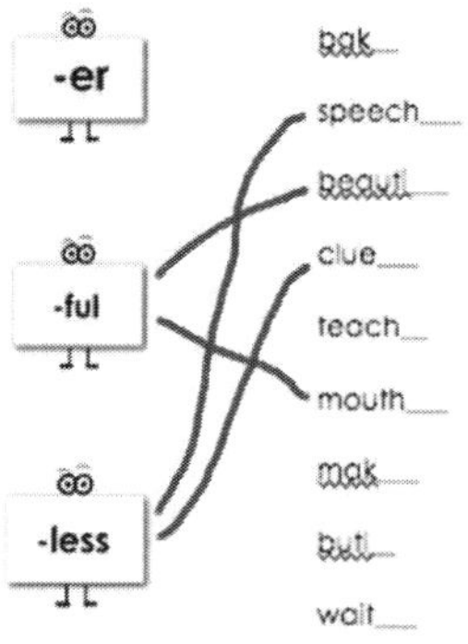

Step 2 Solutions

1. **Full of wonder**: wonder___
   -er -less -ful
2. **Someone who sends**: send___
   -er -less -ful
3. **Without power**: power___
   -er -less -ful
4. **Someone who takes**: tak___
   -er -less -ful
5. **Full of thanks**: thank___
   -er -less -ful

Step 3 Solutions:

speechless	teacher	mouthful
butler	clueless	beautiful
maker	waiter	baker

OFFICIAL GUARDIAN MAIL

Mission 12: Superlatives

Dear guardians and Grammar Games competitors,

We are so sorry we had to interrupt the games, but you may have noticed that something was wrong. We learned that Suffix was able to use yet another virus against us. This time he deleted the **–est** suffix. Without it, we can't declare winners.

We are already working with a programmer, but we need you to put the superlatives where they belong. As soon as you do, the games can begin again!

Sincerely,

Kirk, Luke, and Ellen English

Guardians of Grammar Galaxy

☆ Step 1: On Guard & Choose the Correct Superlative

On Guard. *Highlight the correct answer.*

1. What is a synonym for big?
   large red tiny

2. A new vocabulary word should go in your:
   toy box word book sock drawer

3. Which prefix makes ___**use** a word?
   re- un-

4. A dictionary is an example of what?
   nonfiction fiction

5. In chapter 11, the word tizzy means?
   frustrated panic bored

Say each of these words in a sentence. *Their meanings are given.*

eligible – *qualified* **mesmerized** – *fascinated* **exhilarating** – *excited*

Choose the correct superlative. *Highlight the superlative needed to choose a winner.* ***Hint***: *Use the number of competitors pictured*.

	better best
	faster fastest
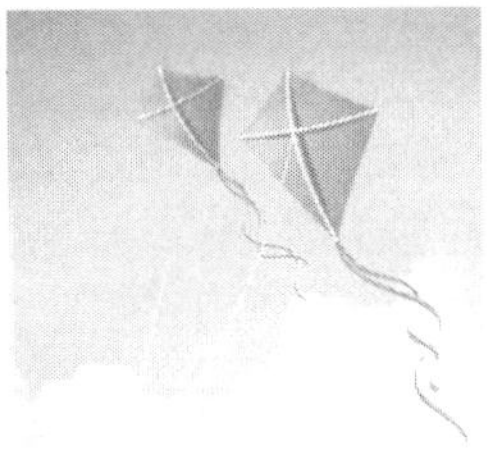	higher highest
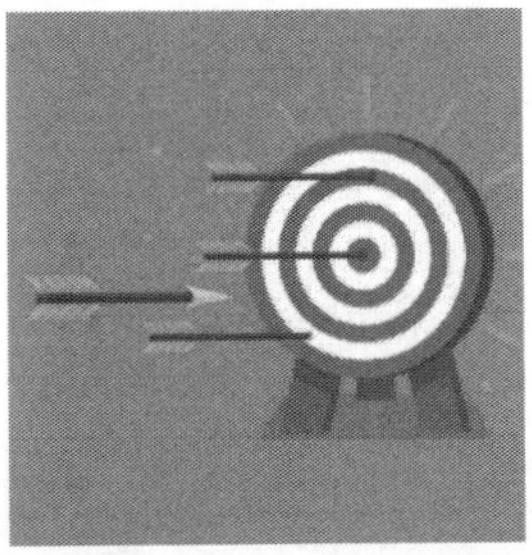	closer closest
	stronger strongest

☆ Step 2: Choose Superlatives in Sentences

Read the sentence. *Highlight the missing superlative suffix or word.*

1. Jake has three brothers. Of all of them, he is the tall___.

   -er -est

2. Ava has one sister. Next to her, she is short___.

   -er -est

3. Ben was mad that his cookie was small___ compared to his brother's.

   -er -est

4. Next year, Emma hopes to do ______ than she did this year.

   better best

5. Of all subjects, Kaden likes math the ______.

   better best

Activity. *How far can you jump? Practice and see if you get* ***better*** *each time. Compare your distance to your family members and see whose jump is* ***best****.* ***Note:*** *If you can't do this, time yourself saying the alphabet backwards and compare.*

☆ Step 3: Use Superlatives in Personal Expression

Highlight which option you like and then highlight if you like it BETTER or BEST depending on how many choices there are.

1. ice cream	chocolate	chips		BETTER	BEST
2. being outside	being inside			BETTER	BEST
3. winter	summer	spring	fall	BETTER	BEST
4. fiction	nonfiction			BETTER	BEST
5. dogs	cats			BETTER	BEST

Vocabulary Victory! *Do you remember what these words mean? Check Step 1 if you forgot.*

eligible **mesmerizing** **exhilarating**

☆ Advanced Guardians Only

Use superlatives in writing. *Write or dictate words to complete each sentence.*

________________________________ is one thing I want to get **better** at than I am now.

________________________________ is something I am **best** at.

OFFICIAL GUARDIAN MAIL

Mission 12: Update

Dear guardians,

You're the best! And we are happy we can write that. We were able to correct the superlative virus and even better, we were able to complete the Grammar Games.

To be honest, I (Luke) hoped to get a gold medal but did not. Father told me that the best prize isn't a medal but doing better than you did before. I plan to train harder for next year and I look forward to competing with you!

That reminds us…you don't have to be the best reader, but you can become a better reader by reading every day. Are you?

We are attaching the solutions to the Superlatives Mission. Did you get them all correct?

Sincerely,

Kirk, Luke, and Ellen English

Guardians of Grammar Galaxy

P.S. We are also attaching the Vocabulary Challenge. You are ready to take it to earn your Vocabulary Star. We know you can do it! Before you take it, you may want to review the information from the guidebook in chapters 8-12.

Step 1 Solutions

On Guard.

1. What is a synonym for big?

large   red   tiny

2. A new vocabulary word should go in your:

toy box   word book   sock drawer

3. Which prefix makes ___**use** a word?

re-   un-

4. A dictionary is an example of what?
nonfiction fiction
5. In chapter 11, the word tizzy means?
frustrated panic bored

Choose the Correct Superlative.

	better best
	faster fastest
	higher highest
	closer closest
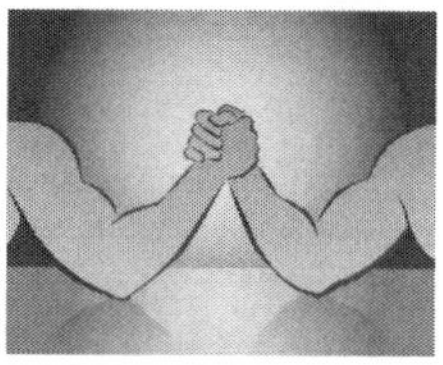	stronger strongest

Step 2 Solutions

1. Jake has three brothers. Of all of them, he is the tall___.
   -er -est
2. Ava has one sister. Next to her, she is short___.
   -er -est
3. Ben was mad that his cookie was small___ compared to his brother's.
   -er -est
4. Next year, Emma hopes to do ______ than she did this year.
   better best
5. Of all subjects, Kaden likes math the ______.
   better best

Step 3 Solutions: *answers will vary*

1. ice cream	chocolate	chips		BETTER	BEST
2. being outside	being inside			BETTER	BEST
3. winter	summer	spring	fall	BETTER	BEST
4. fiction	nonfiction			BETTER	BEST
5. dogs	cats			BETTER	BEST

Vocabulary Challenge I

Carefully read or listen to all the possible answers *and then highlight the letter for the* ***one best answer.***

1. **A synonym is:**
   a. A word that is spelled the same as another word, but has a different meaning
   b. A word that has a similar meaning to another word
   c. A word that rhymes with another word
2. **A book that gives you a list of synonyms for a word is called a:**
   a. thesaurus
   b. brachiosaurus
   c. guidebook
3. **An antonym is a word that means:**
   a. The same thing as another word
   b. A small insect
   c. The opposite of another word
4. **Vocabulary is:**
   a. Words in a language
   b. How many words you know
   c. Words in a language and how many words you know
5. **Good ways to learn new words include:**
   a. Playing video games
   b. Looking up the meaning of words you read
   c. Spending time with a pet
6. **A prefix is:**
   a. A part of a word added at the beginning
   b. A part of a word added at the end
   c. A part of a word added at the beginning or end

7. A suffix is:

a. A part of a word added at the beginning

b. A part of a word added at the end

c. A part of a word added at the beginning or end

8. Prefixes and suffixes:

a. Can change the meanings of words

b. Cannot change the meanings of words

c. Always make words rhyme

9. The superlative -est is a type of:

a. prefix

b. suffix

c. antonym

10. You decide whether to use the ending –er or –est when comparing based on:

a. How tired you are

b. The flip of a coin

c. How many you are comparing

Number Correct:________/10

☆ *Extra Challenge*

How many of these vocabulary words can you remember the meaning of?

engrossed	**infirmary**	**diversity**	**mortified**
grousing	**appease**	**astonished**	**eerily**
replicating	**recounting**	**tizzy**	**withering**
eligible	**mesmerized**	**exhilarating**	

Number Correct:________/15

<u>Vocabulary Challenge 1 Answers</u>

1.b; 2.a; 3.c; 4.c; 5.b; 6.a; 7.b; 8.a; 9.b; 10.c

If you got 9 or more correct, congratulations! You've earned your Vocabulary Star. You can color the star or add a sticker to your Grammar Guardian bookmark. You are ready for an adventure in spelling.

If you did not get 9 or more correct, don't worry. You have another chance. You may want to have your teacher review the information in the guidebook for each story you've read so far. Then take the Vocabulary Challenge 2. Remember to **choose the <u>one</u> best answer**.

<u>Extra Challenge Answers</u>

Here are the meanings of the vocabulary words. Review, say them in a sentence, and see if you can remember more of them.

engrossed – *occupied*	**infirmary** - *hospital*	**diversity** - *variety*
mortified - *ashamed*	**grousing** - *complaining*	**appease** - *please*
astonished - *surprised*	**eerily** - *creepily*	**replicating** – *copying*
recounting - *describing*	**tizzy** - *panic*	**withering** - *dying*
eligible - *qualified*	**mesmerized** - *fascinated*	**exhilarating** - *excited*

Vocabulary Challenge 2

Carefully read or listen to all the possible answers *and then highlight the letter for the* **<u>one</u> best answer.**

1. **A synonym for <u>hot</u> is:**

   a. cool

   b. warm

   c. cool and warm

2. **A thesaurus gives you:**

   a. synonyms

   b. antonyms

   c. synonyms and antonyms

3. **An antonym for <u>good</u> is:**

   a. bad

   b. great

   c. wonderful

4. **You have been using your word book to:**

   a. get out of chores

   b. increase your vocabulary

   c. get better at video games

5. **The more you read, the more you will increase your:**

   a. sleep

   b. vocabulary

   c. height

6. **The prefix of <u>rewind</u> is:**

   a. re-

   b. wind

   c. un-

7. **The suffix of wonderful is:**
   a. wonder
   b. -less
   c. -ful
8. **Which word becomes its antonym by adding un-?**
   a. dog
   b. do
   c. six
9. **Which word is a superlative?**
   a. great
   b. greater
   c. good
10. **Which superlative describes the winner of three runners?**
   a. fastest
   b. faster
   c. fast

Number Correct:________/10

Vocabulary Challenge 2 Answers

1.b; 2.c; 3.a; 4.b; 5.b; 6.a; 7.c; 8.b; 9.b; 10.a

If you got 9 or more correct, congratulations! You've earned your Vocabulary Star. You can color the star or add a sticker to your Grammar Guardian bookmark. You are now ready for an adventure in spelling.

If you did not get 9 or more correct, don't worry. Review the questions you missed with your teacher. You may want to get more practice using the resources at http://GrammarGalaxyBooks.com/Nebula. Your teacher can ask you other questions like the ones you missed and if you get them correct, you'll have earned your Vocabulary Star and can move on to an adventure in spelling.

Unit III: Adventures in Spelling

OFFICIAL GUARDIAN MAIL

Mission 13: Alphabetizing

Dear fellow guardians,

I am sorry to report that we have a problem with all of our digital dictionaries. We aren't sure what's wrong yet, but we hope to get them working again quickly.

Until then, we will have to use printed dictionaries. You should have one for emergencies like this and you should know how to use it. Guardians should know how to find words in dictionaries and how to alphabetize if needed. This mission is required training!

We will update you as soon as possible on the status of our digital dictionaries.

Sincerely,

Ellen English

Guardian of Grammar Galaxy

☆ Step 1: On Guard & Put Objects in Alphabetical Order

On Guard. *Use a highlighter to mark TRUE or FALSE for each question.*

1. The word super is a superlative. TRUE FALSE
2. The word thankless has a prefix. TRUE FALSE
3. Watching TV is the best way to increase your vocabulary. TRUE FALSE
4. A synonym for thankless is suffix. TRUE FALSE
5. Wind and breeze are homographs. TRUE FALSE

Say each of these words in a sentence. *Their meanings are given.*

sheepishly – *guiltily* **emanated** – *came* **farewell** – *good-bye*

Review the alphabet. *Can you sing the song?*

a b c d e f g h i j k l m n o p q r s t u v w x y z

Put the following objects in alphabetical order by name. *Draw a line from the fruit pictures to the order in which their first letter appears in the alphabet.*

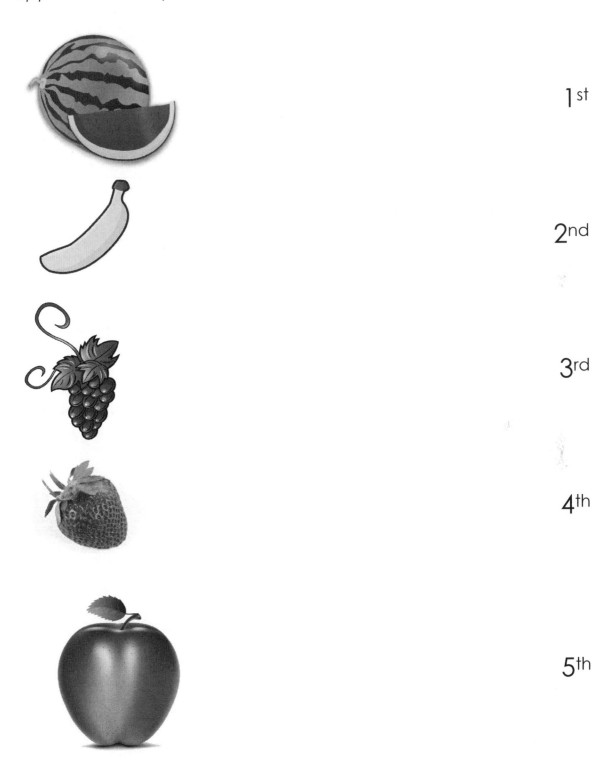

1st

2nd

3rd

4th

5th

☆ Step 2: Identify Words in Alphabetical Order

Which of the following words are NOT in alphabetical order? *Highlight the words that aren't in order by the alphabet.* ***Note:*** *Look at the second or third letters of the word if the first letter or letters are the same. For example, ca**r** comes before ca**t** because **r** is before **t** in the alphabet.*

1. cat	dog	dinosaur
2. goat	horse	sheep
3. boat	car	train
4. fish	flower	frog
5. grass	grow	green

Activity. *Put your family members in order by alphabetizing their first names. Who would be first, second, third, and so on? How does it change if you use* Mom *or* Dad *instead of first names?*

☆ Step 3: Find Words in a Dictionary

Use guide words to find spelling words. *Draw an X over words that you would NOT find on a dictionary page that included these guide words. For the words that do not belong on the page, tell your teacher if you would find the word before or after this page.*

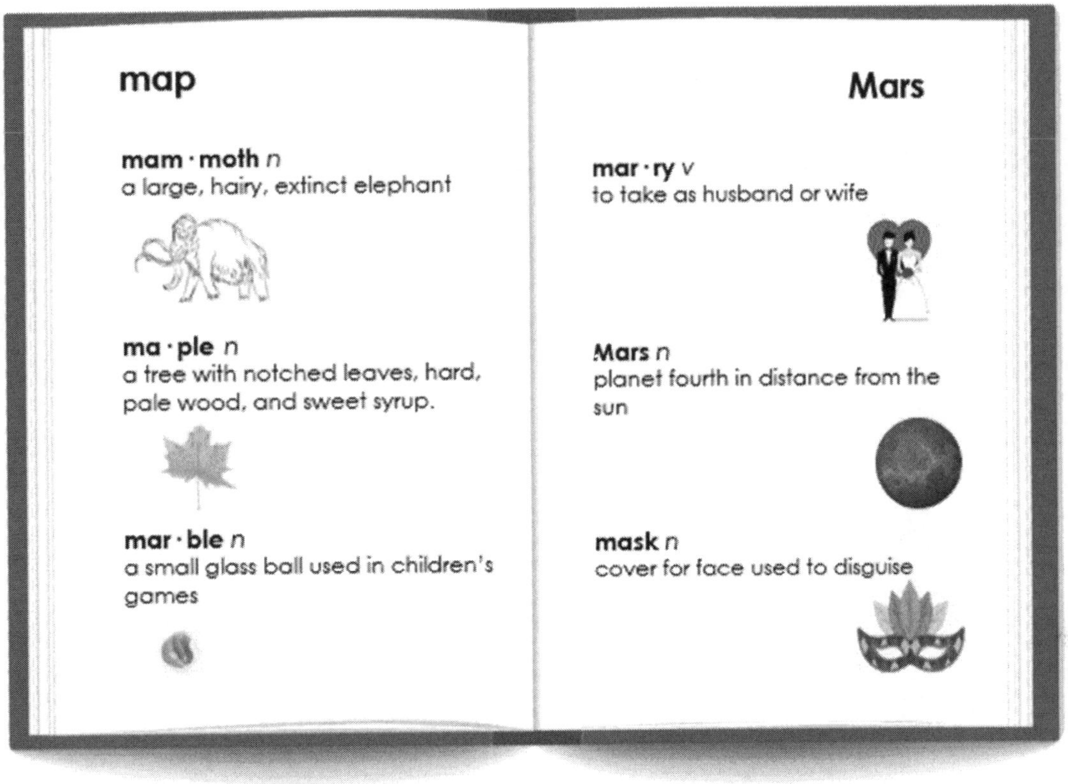
map
mam · moth n
a large, hairy, extinct elephant
ma · ple n
a tree with notched leaves, hard, pale wood, and sweet syrup.
mar · ble n
a small glass ball used in children's games
Mars
mar · ry v
to take as husband or wife
Mars n
planet fourth in distance from the sun
mask n
cover for face used to disguise

Vocabulary Victory! *Do you remember what these words mean? Check Step 1 if you forgot.*

sheepishly **emanated** **farewell**

☆ Advanced Guardians Only

Look up the word guardian in a printed dictionary. *Write down the two guide words you find on the page.*

OFFICIAL GUARDIAN MAIL

Mission 13: Update

Dear guardians,

You will be relieved to hear that the digital dictionaries are working once again! But we are also glad that we have learned to use a printed dictionary, just in case.

We are attaching the answers to this alphabetizing mission and just for fun, we are signing our names alphabetically.

Sincerely,

Ellen, Kirk, and Luke English

Guardians of Grammar Galaxy

P.S. Are you learning new vocabulary words and adding them to your word book?

Step 1 Solutions

On Guard.

1. The word super is a superlative. TRUE FALSE
2. The word thankless has a prefix. TRUE FALSE
3. Watching TV is the best way to increase your vocabulary. TRUE FALSE
4. A synonym for thankless is suffix. TRUE FALSE
5. Wind and breeze are homographs. TRUE FALSE

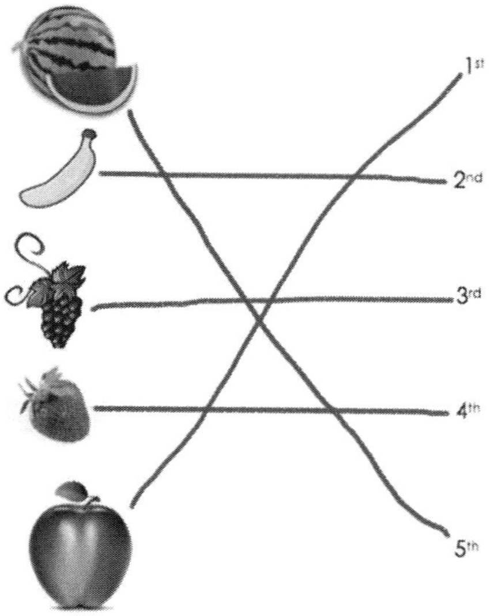
1st
2nd
3rd
4th
5th

Step 2 Solutions

1.	cat	dog	dinosaur
2.	goat	horse	sheep
3.	boat	car	train
4.	fish	flower	frog
5.	grass	grow	green

Step 3 Solutions:

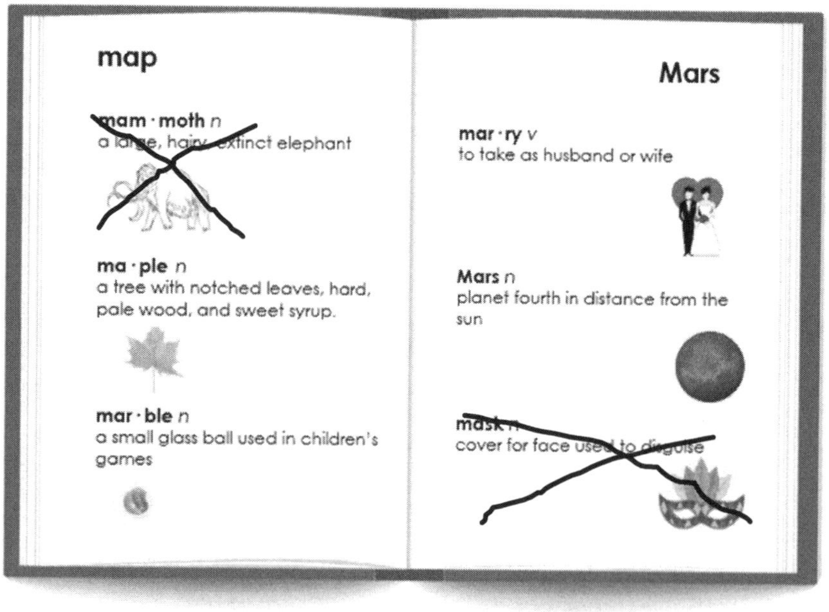
map
mam · moth n
a large, hairy, extinct elephant
ma · ple n
a tree with notched leaves, hard, pale wood, and sweet syrup.
mar · ble n
a small glass ball used in children's games
Mars
mar · ry v
to take as husband or wife
Mars n
planet fourth in distance from the sun
mask n
cover for face used to disguise

Mammoth is found before these pages and *mask* is found after.

OFFICIAL GUARDIAN MAIL

Mission 14: Syllables

Dear guards,

You may know that we have a prob—. We can't write or say words with more than one syll—, sound. We need you to fix it! Find words with more than one sound, so we can get them out of Mums— where they can't be used. The king is going to have Word World shut down if words with more than one syll— aren't let in.

Thank you, friends!

Yours,

Kirk, Luke and Elln Eng-

Guards of Gram—Gal—

☆ Step 1: On Guard & Choose Multi-Syllable Pictures

On Guard. *Highlight the correct answer for each statement.*

1. Which word would appear first in the dictionary?

   guardian guest

2. Guide words appear in a:

   digital dictionary printed dictionary

3. The following is a suffix:

   -ful re-

4. Which prefix means to do again?

   pre- re-

5. When comparing two people, use the superlative:

   better best

Say each of these words in a sentence. *Their meanings are given.*

distress – *upset* **gibberish** – *nonsense* **liberty** – *freedom*

Choose multi-syllable pictures. *Circle the pictures of words that have more than one syllable that were not allowed into Word World.*

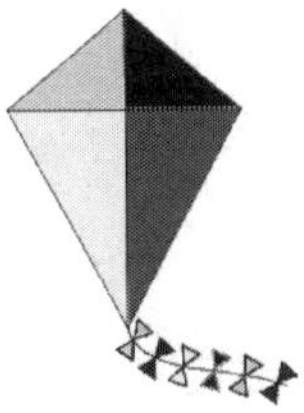

☆ Step 2: Count Syllables

Count the sounds. *Highlight the number of syllables in each word. Have your teacher read them if you need help.* ***Hint****:* *Put down a finger for each sound you hear.*

1. **Exasperated**

   1 2 3 4 5
2. **Gibberish**

   1 2 3 4 5
3. **Liberty**

   1 2 3 4 5
4. **Vocabulary**

   1 2 3 4 5
5. **Syllable**

   1 2 3 4 5

Activity. *Roll a die and say a word that has the number of syllables you rolled. You can make it a competition by trying to be the first to say a word when the number comes up. If you can't think of six-syllable words, ask your teacher to help you check http://GrammarGalaxyBooks.com/Nebula.*

☆ Step 3: Haiku

Find the correct haiku. *A correctly written haiku poem has five syllables in the first line, seven in the second, and five in the third. Write how many syllables are in each line in the box on the right. Then put an X on the poem that doesn't have the 5-7-5 syllable pattern. Ask your teacher for help if you need it.*

Trees blossom in spring		**Birds lay eggs in the spring**	
And lose their leaves in the fall.		**And fly south in the fall.**	
They rest in winter.		**I miss them in winter.**	

Vocabulary Victory! *Do you remember what these words mean? Check Step 1 if you forgot.*

distress **gibberish** **liberty**

☆ Advanced Guardians Only

Finish the haiku poem. *Add words in the blanks that give the poem five syllables in the first line, seven in the second, and five in the third. Write or dictate the words and ask for help with spelling if you need it.* ***Hint:*** *Count how many syllables are already in each line. Then add a word that has the number of syllables that are left.*

I look up at ______________________

in the ______________________________ blue sky

and I am ___________________________.

OFFICIAL GUARDIAN MAIL

Mission 14: Update

Dear guardians,

We presented the ticket taker at Word World with an order from the king stating that words with more than one syllable must be allowed in. With your help, we also found words that had been turned away and went to Mumsville. We apologized and invited them back to Word World. Most of them returned!

There may be a few stragglers left in Mumsville, so we will ask you to find them in the weeks ahead. For now, it's so great to be able to use words with more than one syllable!

Thanks so much. We are sending you the solutions to this mission, just in case.

Sincerely,

Kirk, Luke, and Ellen English

Guardians of Grammar Galaxy

Step 1 Solutions

On Guard.

1. Which word would appear first in the dictionary?
   guardian guest
2. Guide words appear in a:
   digital dictionary **printed dictionary**
3. The following is a suffix:
   -ful re-
4. Which prefix means to do again?
   pre- **re-**
5. When comparing two people, use the superlative:
   better best

Step 2 Solutions

1. **Exasperated**
   1 2 3 4 5
2. **Gibberish**
   1 2 3 4 5
3. **Liberty**
   1 2 3 4 5
4. **Vocabulary**
   1 2 3 4 5
5. **Syllable**
   1 2 3 4 5

Step 3 Solutions:

Trees blossom in spring	5	**Birds lay eggs in the spring**	6
And lose their leaves in the fall.	7	**And fly south in the fall.**	6
They rest in winter.	5	**I miss them in winter.**	6

....

OFFICIAL GUARDIAN MAIL

Mission 15: Phonics

Attention guardians!

I can't spend a lot of time writing this mission because I could get caught. I am at the Word Academy where General Arnold is keeping letters and diagraphs (blends) from making their sounds. In order to keep all the beginning readers reading, I am having to review all these sounds myself—that is, until the king can stop the general.

Anyway, that's where you come in. If you can help me say the phonics sounds, I can get some rest. I won't lie. It's hard work!

Thanks, guys!

Sincerely,

Luke English

Guardian of Grammar Galaxy

☆ Step 1: On Guard & Identify Beginning Phonics

On Guard. *Answer the questions for your teacher.*

1. Say the alphabet.

2. How many syllables are in supercalifragilisticexpialidocious (from *Mary Poppins*)?

3. Which of the following change the meanings of words: prefixes or suffixes?

4. What is an antonym for after?

5. What is a nonfiction book?

Say each of these words in a sentence. *Their meanings are given.*

disciplined – *trained* **chaperones** – *guides* **insignias** – *symbols*

Identify beginning phonics. *Highlight the letter that starts the name of each picture and say the sound the letter makes.*

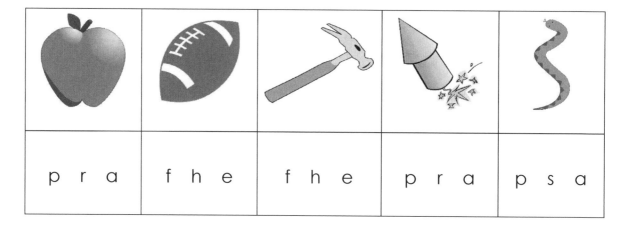

		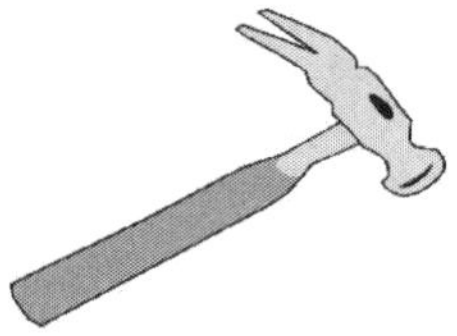		
p r a	f h e	f h e	p r a	p s a

☆ Step 2: Review Letter Sounds

Draw the correct mark over the <u>first</u> vowel. *Write ¯ over the long vowels that say their names and ˘ over the vowels that have a short sound. The first one is done for you.*

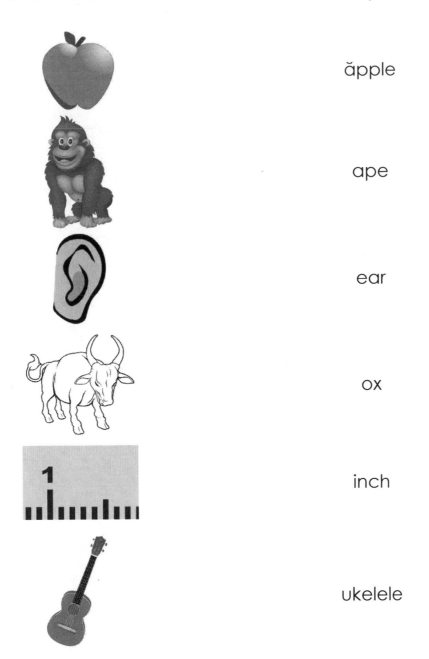

ăpple

ape

ear

ox

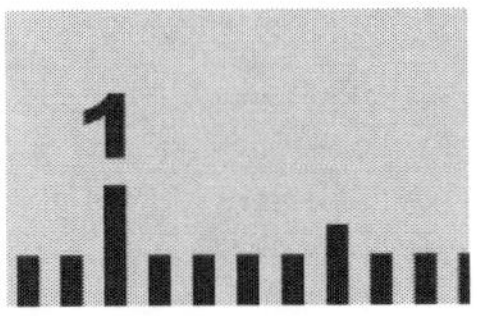

inch

ukelele

Activity. *Say the sounds for each letter below. Can you name the picture for each letter too? For example, say ă as in ant. Have your teacher time you the first time through and then try it again. Did you do it faster?* ***Note***: *In this list, g has a soft sound. Do you know what its hard sound is? You'll hear it when you say gorilla. The short sound of u is in umbrella bird. Say their names and sounds when you reach the end of the alphabet.*

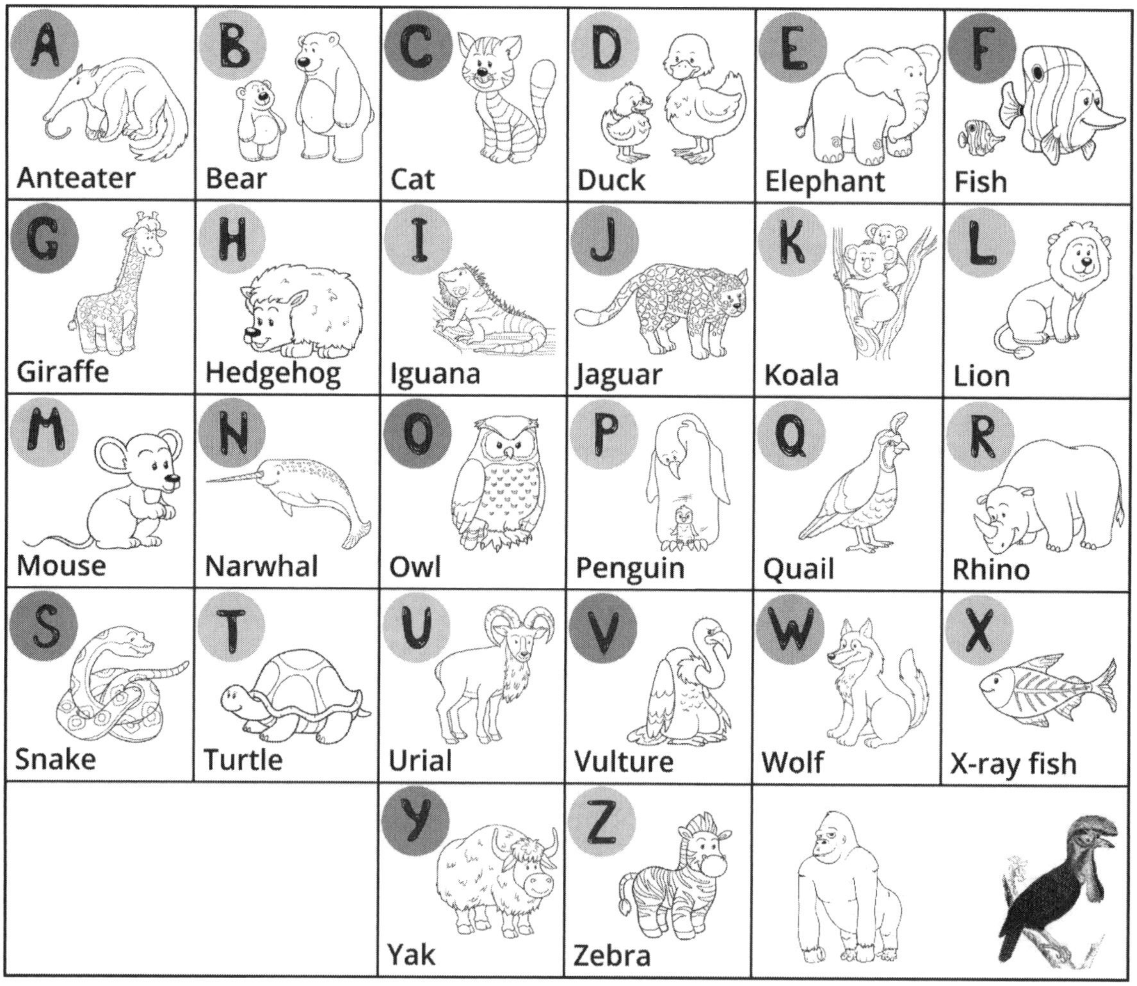

☆ Step 3: Review Blends

Say the blend and a word that includes it. *For example, say bl—as in black.* ***Hint:*** *If you can't think of a word, try a dictionary!*

bl	**cl**	**fl**
gl	**pl**	**sl**
br	**cr**	**dr**
fr	**gr**	**gr**
pr	**tr**	**sc**
sm	**sn**	**sp**
st	**sw**	**tw**

Vocabulary Victory! *Do you remember what these words mean? Check Step 1 if you forgot.*

disciplined **chaperones** **insignias**

☆ Advanced Guardians Only

Write or dictate a sentence using more than one of the blends in Step 3.

OFFICIAL GUARDIAN MAIL

Mission 15: Update

Dear guardians,

You guys are the best! Because you were busy reviewing the phonics sounds, I was able to take a break. I was even able to nab a snack from the mess hall when no one was looking.

The best news, though, is that General Arnold is no longer in charge and the sound-offs are happening once again. I got to see one before I went home and it was so cool!

Thanks again! Oh, and Kirk reminded me that I should give you the solutions to the mission, so here they are.

Sincerely,

Luke English

Guardian of Grammar Galaxy

Step 1 Solutions

On Guard.

1. **Say the alphabet.** a b c d e f g h i j k l m n o p q r s t u v w x y z
2. **How many syllables are in supercalifragilisticexpialidocious?** (from *Mary Poppins*)? 14.
3. **Which of the following change the meanings of words: prefixes or suffixes?** Both do.
4. **What is an antonym for after?** Before.
5. **What is a nonfiction book?** A factual book.

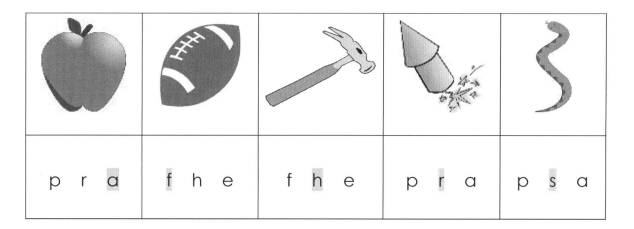

		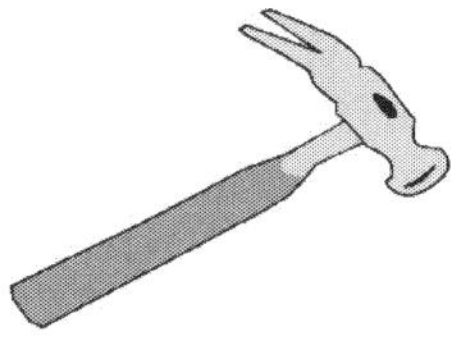	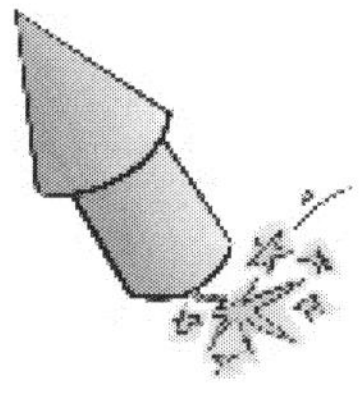	
p r a	f h e	f h e	p r a	p s a

Step 2 Solutions

āpe, ēar, ŏx, ĭnch, ūkelele

OFFICIAL GUARDIAN MAIL

Mission 16: Spelling with Phonics

Dear friends,

We don't know if you have noticed yet, but spell-check programs aren't working. The last edition of the newspaper was almost impossible to read.

The king pointed out that spell checkers don't help us to spell everything correctly. We need to know different methods for remembering how words are spelled. The easiest and most important way to spell is using phonics.

Please complete the following mission while we try to get spell checkers working again.

Sincerely,

Kirk, Luke, and Ellen English

Guardians of Grammar Galaxy

☆ Step 1: On Guard & Phonics Diagraphs

On Guard. *Highlight the correct answer.*

1. Which of the following words uses the blend **sh**?
   which that wish

2. Which of the following has the syllables marked correctly?
   vocab-u-lary vo-cab-u-lar-y voc-ab-ul-ary

3. Which word would come first in the dictionary?
   bat baby cap

4. The word unbelief has a:
   prefix suffix

5. Which word is a synonym for boat?
   plane jet ship

Say each of these words in a sentence. *Their meanings are given.*

erupted – *exploded* **vice** – *badness* **incredulous** – *unbelieving*

Phonics digraphs. *Review the sounds these seven digraphs make with your teacher. Highlight every word you are able to read that has this blend. Can you think of any other words that include the blend?*

th *note the two sounds*	that, then, them, than, this
	with, thin
ch	much, such, children
sh	short, fish, ship
wh	when, which
ng	long, song, king, sing, thing, bring
nk *sounds like ngk*	think, rink, pink

☆ Step 2: Spelling with Phonics

Which of these words are misspelled? *Highlight them.* **Hint:** *Words should be spelled using phonics, as you expect.*

had muuch

but not

cann ann

if uup

thewn them

Activity. *Don't peek! Have your teacher spell the following words out loud. Say the word that was spelled. How many of them did you know?*

1. in 2. fish 3. that 4. it 5. for 6. on 7. with 8. at 9. this 10. or

☆ Step 3: Spell Words Using Phonics

Spell words using phonics. *Don't peek! Your teacher will give you a word to spell using phonics. Tell your teacher what letters to write on a dry erase board or notebook to make the word. If you make a mistake, have your teacher erase it.*

1. sit 2. man 3. help 4. got 5. cup

If you missed any, look at the words and try again until you can spell them. If you got them all correct, have your teacher give you these. Don't peek!

1. song 2. fish 3. blast 4. such 5. step

Vocabulary Victory! *Do you remember what these words mean? Check Step 1 if you forgot.*

erupted **vice** **incredulous**

☆ Advanced Guardians Only

Write phonics spelling words as your teacher gives them to you. *Don't peek! Have your teacher give you the words while you use a dry erase board or paper to spell them.*

1. set 2. end 3. must 4. big 5. Went

6. men 7. land 8. us 9. hand 10. last

OFFICIAL GUARDIAN MAIL

Mission 16: Update

Dear guardians,

Unfortunately, our spell checkers still aren't working! Our father says he won't read the newspaper until they're fixed. He also said that we will have to keep reviewing phonics and learning to spell using them. We told him that we will do whatever it takes to guard the galaxy!

Attached are the solutions to the mission you completed. How did you do?

Sincerely,

Kirk, Luke, and Ellen English

Guardians of Grammar Galaxy

Step 1 Solutions

On Guard.

1. Which of the following words uses the blend **sh**?
   which　　that　　wish
2. Which of the following has the syllables marked correctly?
   vocab-u-lary　　vo-cab-u-lar-y　　voc-ab-ul-ary
3. Which word would come first in the dictionary?
   bat　　baby　　cap
4. The word unbelief has a:
   prefix　　suffix
5. Which word is a synonym for boat?
   plane　　jet　　ship

Step 2 Solutions

had	muuch
but	not
cann	ann

if	uup
thewn	them

OFFICIAL GUARDIAN MAIL

Mission 17: Compound Words

Dear guardian guys and gals,

Yes, we are writing with another mission. This time compound words—two words that have been made one—have been separated by mistake. We need you to find them and put them back together before the things these words describe disappear.

You'll learn that this is a really important mission!

Sincerely,

Kirk, Luke, and Ellen English

Guardians of Grammar Galaxy

☆ Step 1: On Guard & Is It a Compound Word?

On Guard. *Highlight the correct answer.*

1. Which of these words is spelled correctly?
   stop	stowp	stip

2. Phonics review is most important for:
   beginning readers	generals	zoo animals

3. To write a haiku, you need to count:
   to ten	syllables	sheep

4. To find a word's spelling, you need a:
   fiction book	newspaper	dictionary

5. A problem and solution in a story is also called the:
   setting	plot	tall tale

Say each of these words in a sentence. *Their meanings are given.*

diverted – *distracted*　**bolstered** – *strengthened*　**deflated** – *discouraged*

Is it a compound word? Does the picture represent a compound word? *Highlight YES or NO.*

YES
NO

YES
NO

YES
NO

YES
NO

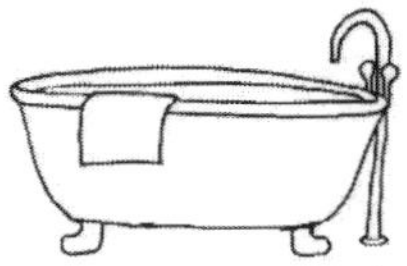

YES
NO

☆ Step 2: Match Words to Make Compound Words

Choose a word to form a compound word. *Draw lines from a word on the left to a word on the right to form correct words.* ***Hint:*** *Some words on the left may fit with more than one word on the right. If you aren't sure, check a dictionary.*

any	day
out	one
my	self
in	thing
to	side

Activity. *Which word do you think you could you make the most compound words out of: back or some? After you've guessed, count how many words you can think of for each. When you run out of ideas, ask your teacher for more. Which word made the most compound words?*

☆ Step 3: Find the Separated Compound Words

Use a curved line to connect two words that should be one word in the following paragraph. *The first one is done for you. Get help reading if you need it.*

> On his birth day, Sam's mom asked him what he wanted to be some day. He made a list of fun jobs: cow boy, fire man, and life guard. He also wanted to play foot ball. He wanted to do any thing that would be out side.

Vocabulary Victory! *Do you remember what these words mean? Check Step 1 if you forgot.*

diverted **bolstered** **deflated**

Spelling Success *Have your teacher spell the following words, while you draw a picture that shows you know what the spelled word is on a dry erase board or on paper. Don't peek!*

1. ten 2. big 3. hand 4. plant 5. stop

☆ Advanced Guardians Only

Write or dictate a sentence about which compound word you would not want to disappear and why.

OFFICIAL GUARDIAN MAIL

Mission 17: Update

Dear guardians,

With your help, we think we have most of the compound words back together. Luke is glad because he still wants to play spaceball and he loves blueberry muffins. The king reversed the order that caused the problem.

We are pretty sure you completed your mission correctly, but we are sending you the solutions anyway.

Sincerely,

Kirk, Luke, and Ellen English

Guardians of Grammar Galaxy

P.S. Are you still reading every day? Keep a lookout for compound words as you read. It's amazing how many of them there are!

Step 1 Solutions

On Guard.

1. Which of these words is spelled correctly?
   stop stowp stip
2. Phonics review is most important for:
   beginning readers generals zoo animals
3. To write a haiku, you need to count:
   to ten **syllables** sheep
4. To find a word's spelling, you need a:
   fiction book newspaper **dictionary**
5. A problem and solution in a story is also called the:
   setting **plot** tall tale

Is it a compound word?

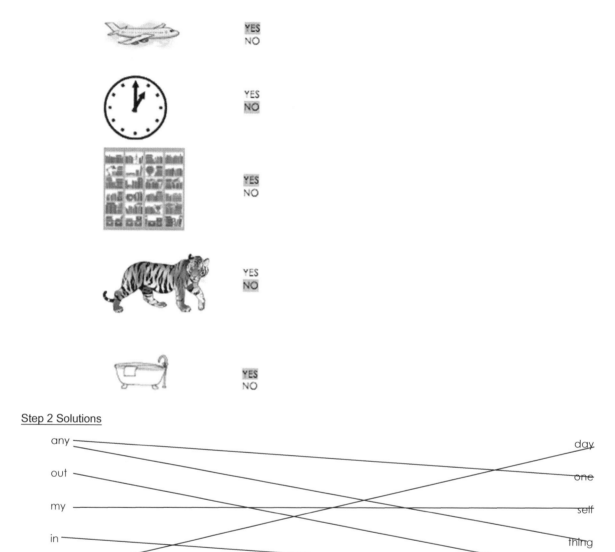

YES
NO

YES
NO

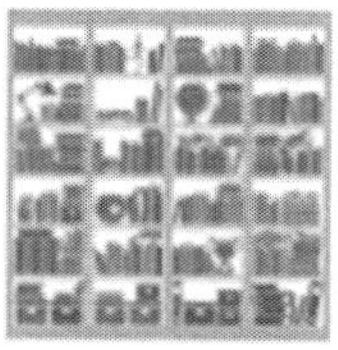

YES
NO

YES
NO

YES
NO

Step 2 Solutions

any	day
out	one
my	self
in	thing
to	side

Step 3 Solutions:

On his birth day, Sam's mom asked him what he wanted to be some day. He made a list of fun jobs: cow boy, fire man, and life guard. He also wanted to play foot ball. He wanted to do any thing that would be out side.

OFFICIAL GUARDIAN MAIL

Mission 18: Contractions

Dear fellow guardians,

We think you are probably just as big of fans of the show *Contraction Nation* as we are. That's what makes this mission hard. Apostrophe Ink has been adding apostrophes to words that shouldn't have them. A contraction is a shortened form of a word in which an apostrophe takes the place of missing letters.

Your main mission is to undo the apostrophes that don't belong. If we don't remove them, our citizens will get confused.

Thanks in advance for your hard work!

Sincerely,

Kirk, Luke, and Ellen English

Guardians of Grammar Galaxy

Step 1: On Guard & Create Contractions

On Guard. *Highlight TRUE or FALSE for each statement.*

1. Compound words are words that have been used together a lot. TRUE FALSE
2. Spelling can be tricky because English includes many foreign words. TRUE FALSE
3. If you don't know your phonics, you may have trouble reading. TRUE FALSE
4. Knowing syllables in a word can help you spell it. TRUE FALSE
5. Guide words are words that give tours on planet Spelling. TRUE FALSE

Say each of these words in a sentence. *Their meanings are given.*

transformation – *change* **indulged** – *spoiled* **somber** – *gloomy*

Spelling Success. *Have your teacher spell these words using a finger on your back. Can you guess them?* *<u>Don't peek!</u>*

1. us 2. at 3. no 4. me 5. in

Create contractions. *The contractions above are correct. For each set of words below, create a contraction. Add correction fluid/tape or use a white gel pen to remove the letters that do not belong. Then add an apostrophe where it belongs.* **Note**: *You may need to let the fluid/ink dry before adding an apostrophe*.

1. didnot
2. youare
3. Iam
4. wewill
5. itis

Step 2: Remove Apostrophes That Don't Belong

Find incorrect apostrophes. *Use correction fluid/tape or use a white gel pen to remove apostrophes from words that aren't contractions.* ***Hint:*** *You may need to review the list of contractions in Chapter 18.*

haven't	won't	ben't	can't
I'll	wi'll	we'll	fi‘ll
ha've	we've	I've	ga've

Activity. *Try not to use any contractions for the next 30 minutes. How many times do you slip and use them? Have your teacher keep track.*

☆ Step 3: Write contractions

Write the contraction across from the words that want to be shortened. *Remember the apostrophe!*

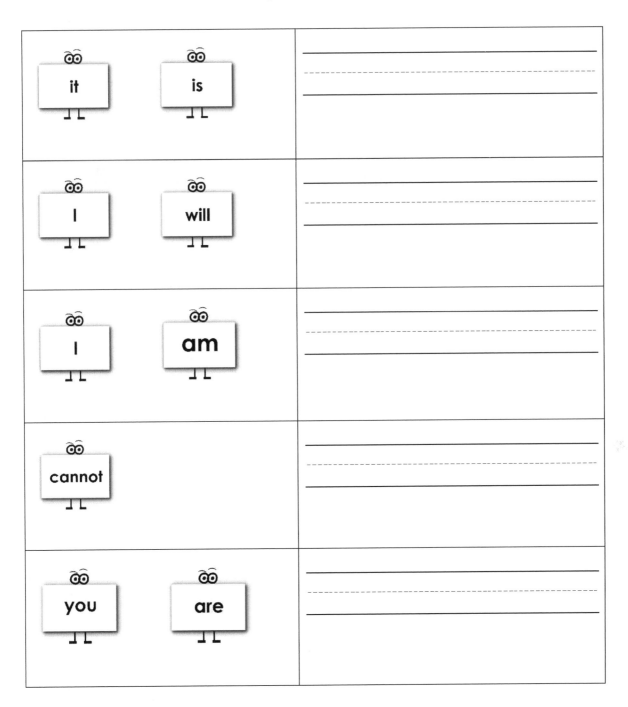

it is	
I will	
I am	
cannot	
you are	

Vocabulary Victory! *Do you remember what these words mean? Check Step 1 if you forgot.*

transformation **indulged** **somber**

☆ Advanced Guardians Only

Write or dictate a sentence using as many contractions as you can.

OFFICIAL GUARDIAN MAIL

Mission 18: Update

Dear guardians,

We haven't got a lot of time, so we'll use contractions. We're sure you're doing everything correctly, because we can't find any apostrophes that don't belong.

The sad news is that *Contraction Nation* isn't going to be on Spelling Network anymore. But at least we won't be confused.

Your solutions are attached.

Sincerely,

Kirk, Luke, and Ellen English

Guardians of Grammar Galaxy

<u>Step 1 Solutions</u>

On Guard.

1.	Compound words are words that have been used together a lot.	TRUE	FALSE
2.	Spelling can be tricky because English includes many foreign words.	TRUE	FALSE
3.	If you don't know your phonics, you may have trouble reading.	TRUE	FALSE
4.	Knowing syllables in a word can help you spell it.	TRUE	FALSE
5.	Guide words are words that give tours on planet Spelling.	TRUE	FALSE

Create contractions.

1. d i d n ' t
2. y o u ' r e
3. I ' m
4. w e ' l l
5. i t ' s

Step 2 Solutions

haven't	won't	ben t	can't
I'll	wi ll	we'll	fi ll
ha ve	we've	I've	ga ve

Step 3 Solutions:

it is	it's
I will	I'll
I am	I'm
cannot	can't
you are	you're

....

OFFICIAL GUARDIAN MAIL

Mission 19: Abbreviations

Dear guardians,

Once again, a Spelling Network program is causing problems. Words that can't be abbreviated have been going to Abbreviation Ink to be shortened with a period. The problem is that not all of them can be abbreviations. If we don't fix them, everyone will be confused, especially the mail service!

We are on our way to planet Spelling. We will explain the problem to Inky and we hope she will help us out. Until then, we need you to find and fix the words that have gotten periods that shouldn't have them.

We will send you a status update soon.

Sincerely,

Kirk, Luke, and Ellen English

Guardians of Grammar Galaxy

☆ Step 1: On Guard & Match Abbreviations

On Guard. *Answer the following questions for your teacher.*

1. What does an apostrophe stand for in a contraction?
2. Give an example of a compound word.
3. Spell a word that you love.
4. Say the short and long sound of each vowel.
5. Is chapter 19 a tall tale? Why or why not?

Say each of these words in a sentence. *Their meanings are given.*

frazzled – *weary* **boulevard** – *road* **gesturing** – *pointing*

Spelling Success. *Use letter tiles from a game or print some from http://GrammarGalaxyBooks.com/Nebula to spell the following words as your teacher says them. No peeking!*

1. last 2. left 3. run 4. next 5. got

Match abbreviations. *These words have been correctly abbreviated. Please match each abbreviation to the picture word it stands for by drawing a line between them.*

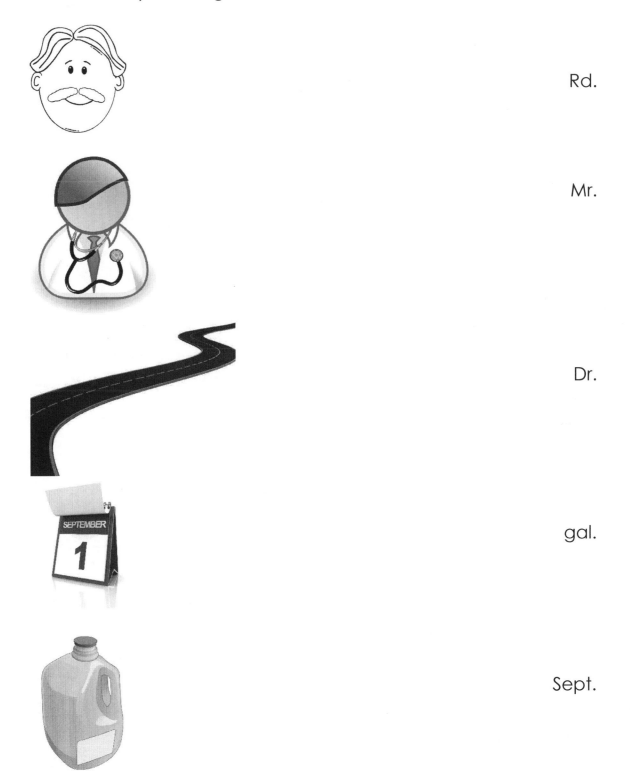

Rd.

Mr.

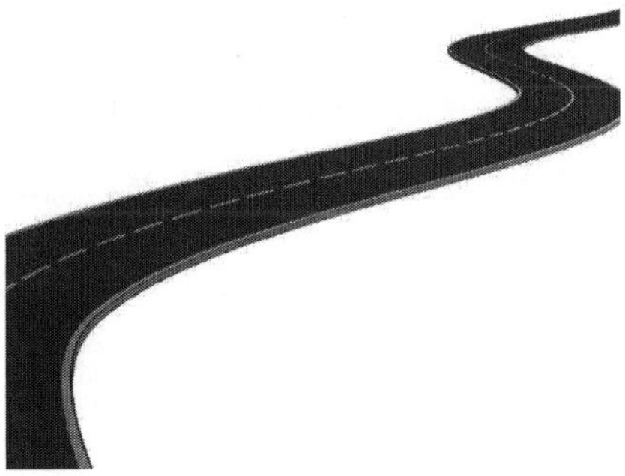

Dr.

gal.

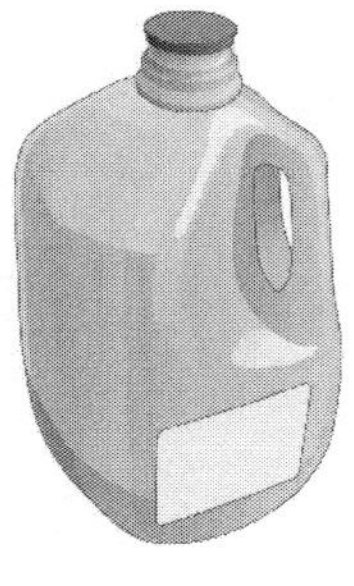

Sept.

☆ Step 2: Find and Fix Incorrect Abbreviations

Correct abbreviations. *If an abbreviation below is incorrect, use correction fluid or tape or a white gel pen to remove letters or periods that don't belong.* ***Hint:*** *Review the list of abbreviations from Chapter 19.*

March – March.	**Mount** – Mt.	**Captain** – Capt.
United States – U.S.	**Corporation** – Corpor.	**wish** – wish.
Saint – St.	**versus** – vs.	**inch** – inch.

Activity. *Initials, which are the first letter of each of a person's names followed by a period, are a form of an abbreviation. What are your initials? As you talk for the next 30 minutes, only use people's initials and not their names.*

☆ Step 3: Create Correct Abbreviations

Create an abbreviation of each word. *Use correction fluid or tape or a white gel pen to remove letters that are not in the abbreviation of each word. Add a period to the end.* ***Hint:*** *If you use fluid or a pen, you may need to wait for it to dry before adding a period.*

December Street Junior foot Friday

Vocabulary Victory! *Do you remember what these words mean? Check Step 1 if you forgot.*

frazzled **boulevard** **gesturing**

☆ Advanced Guardians Only

Rewrite the address below using abbreviations on the blank envelope.

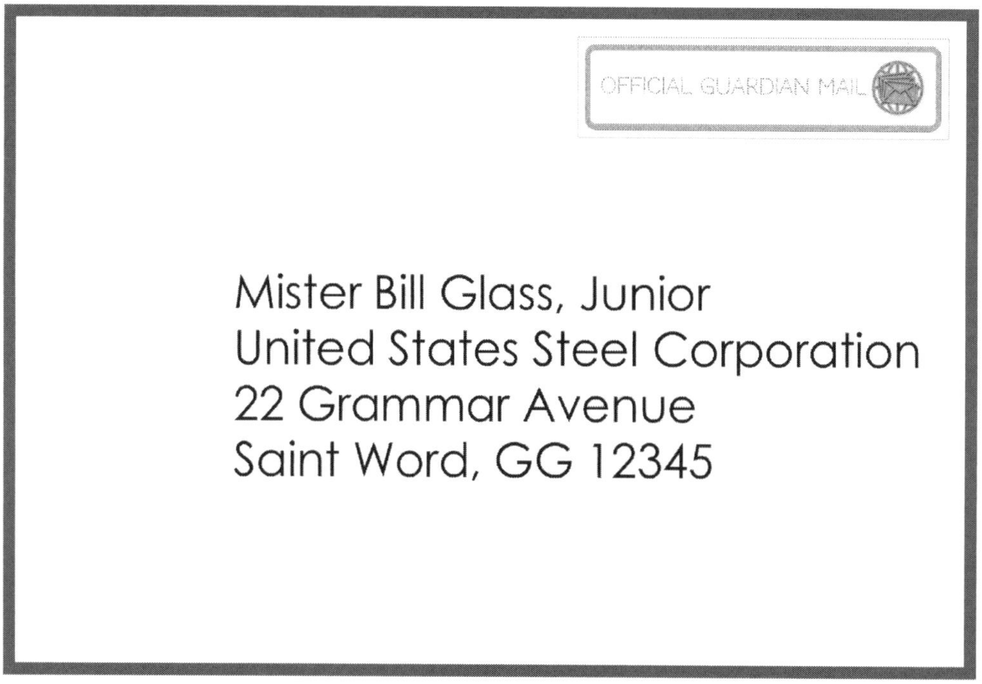

OFFICIAL GUARDIAN MAIL

Mission 19: Update

Dear guardians,

We are happy and sad as we update you. First, we are happy that with your help, we have fixed most of the words that were wrongly abbreviated. We are sad because our new friend Inky has to quit doing something she loved. We have promised her that we will help her look for another job.

We need you to keep looking for incorrect abbreviations, just in case we didn't find them all. Attached are the solutions to the mission we sent you. We have to abbreviate this letter, so we will say good-bye for now.

Sincerely,

Kirk, Luke, and Ellen English

Guardians of Grammar Galaxy

P.S. You have qualified to take the Spelling Challenge. We know you can do it! (P.S. is an abbreviation, remember?)

Step 1 Solutions

On Guard.

1. **What does an apostrophe stand for in a contraction?** Missing letters.
2. **Give an example of a compound word**. Answers will vary.
3. **Spell a word that you love**. Answers will vary.
4. **Say the short and long sound of each vowel.** a e i o u short sounds and then letter names.
5. **Is Chapter 19 a tall tale? Why or why not?** No. Tall tales are written like nonfiction. Chapter 19 is fiction that includes some factual information.

Match Abbreviations.

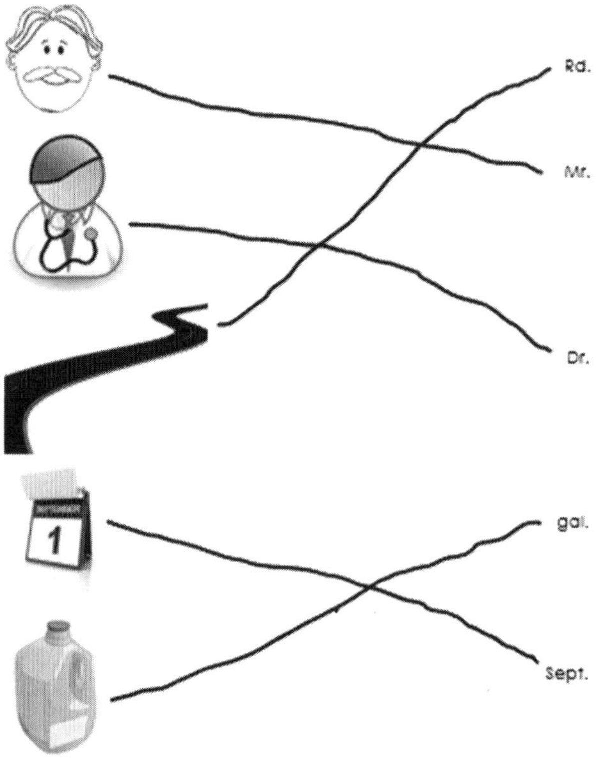

Step 2 Solutions

March – Mar.	**Mount** – Mt.	**Captain** – Capt.
United States – U.S.	**Corporation** – Corp.	**wish** – wish
Saint – St.	**versus** – vs.	**inch** – in.

Step 3 Solutions:

Dec. St. J r. f t. Fri.

Advanced Guardians.

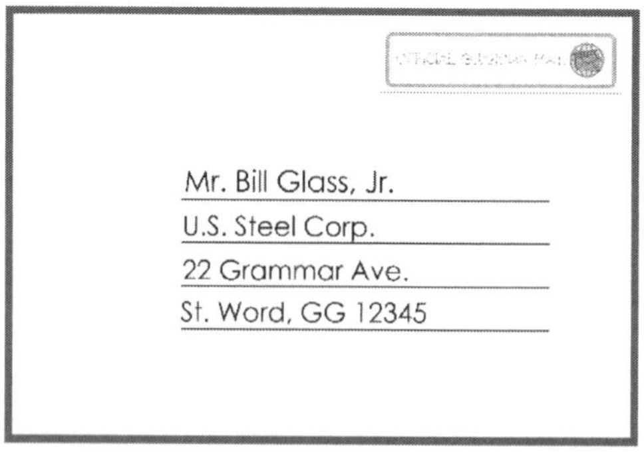

Spelling Challenge I

***Carefully read or listen to all the possible answers** and then highlight the letter for the <u>one</u> **best answer**.*

1. You have to know <u>what</u> to find words in a dictionary?

a. The order of the alphabet

b. The first letter or letters of a word

c. Both the order of the alphabet and the first letter(s) of a word

2. The following words are in alphabetical order:

a. bat, cat, car

b. dog, done, donut

c. ear, eat, dust

3. The following word has two syllables:

a. mother

b. stick

c. wonderful

4. A syllable is:

a. a word that means the same as another word

b. a beat or sound in a word

c. a silly word

5. Phonics is the study of:

a. the shapes of letters

b. abbreviations

c. the sounds letters make

6. Learning phonics will help you:

a. dance

b. spell

c. sleep

7. The word <u>anything</u> is:

a. a homograph

b. an antonym

c. a compound word

8. The following word is <u>not</u> a correct contraction:

a. ha've

b. I've

c. we've

9. Contractions use which punctuation mark?

a. a period

b. an apostrophe

c. a question mark

10. Which word is <u>not</u> a correct abbreviation?

a. Blvd.

b. Rd.

c. Strt.

Number Correct:________/10

☆ *Extra Challenge*

How many of these vocabulary words can you remember the meaning of?

sheepishly	**emanated**	**farewell**	**distress**
gibberish	**liberty**	**disciplined**	**chaperones**
insignias	**erupted**	**vice**	**incredulous**
diverted	**bolstered**	**deflated**	**transformation**
indulged	**somber**	**frazzled**	**boulevard**
gesturing			

Number Correct:________/21

Spelling Challenge 1 Answers

1.c; 2.b; 3.a; 4.b; 5.c; 6.b; 7.c; 8.a; 9.b; 10.c

If you got 9 or more correct, congratulations! You've earned your Spelling Star. You can color the star or add a sticker to your Grammar Guardian bookmark. You are ready for an adventure in grammar.

If you did not get 9 or more correct, don't worry. You have another chance. You may want to have your teacher review the information from each chapter you've read so far. Then take the Spelling Challenge 2. Remember to **choose the one best answer**.

Extra Challenge Answers

Here are the meanings of the vocabulary words. Review, say them in a sentence, and see if you can remember more of them.

sheepishly - *guiltily*	**emanated** - *came*	**farewell** - *good-bye*
distress - *upset*	**gibberish** - *nonsense*	**liberty** - *freedom*
disciplined - *trained*	**chaperones** - *guides*	**insignias** - *symbols*
erupted - *exploded*	**vice** - *badness*	**incredulous** - *unbelieving*
diverted - *distracted*	**bolstered** - *strengthened*	**deflated** – *discouraged*
transformation - *change*	**indulged** - *spoiled*	**somber** – *gloomy*
frazzled - *weary*	**boulevard** - *road*	**gesturing** - *pointing*

Spelling Challenge 2

Carefully read or listen to all the possible answers *and then highlight the letter for the* ***one best answer.***

1. **Which word would you expect to find on a dictionary page with the guide words fish and flat?**
   a. flip
   b. film
   c. flag
2. **Which word comes before shark in the dictionary?**
   a. ship
   b. seed
   c. star
3. **The word afternoon has how many syllables?**
   a. one
   b. two
   c. three
4. **Which letter is unexpected in the word sign based on sound?**
   a. g
   b. i
   c. n
5. **Which of the following is a compound word?**
   a. everybody
   b. breakfast
   c. both everybody and breakfast
6. **Which word is not written correctly?**
   a. airplane
   b. any one
   c. outside

7. In a contraction, the apostrophe takes the place of:

a. a homograph

b. missing letters

c. a period

8. The correct contraction for <u>you are</u> is:

a. your

b. you're

c. your'e

9. The correct abbreviation for <u>Doctor</u> is:

a. Dr.

b. Doc.

c. Doct.

10. Which address is abbreviated correctly?

a. 12345 Hill Road.

b. 12345 Hill Ave.

c. 12345 Hill Strt.

Number Correct:________/10

Spelling Challenge 2 Answers

1.c; 2.b; 3.c; 4.a; 5.c; 6.b; 7.b; 8.b; 9.a; 10.b

If you got 9 or more correct, congratulations! You've earned your Spelling Star. You can color the star or add a sticker to your Grammar Guardian bookmark. You are now ready for an adventure in grammar.

If you did not get 9 or more correct, don't worry. Review the questions you missed with your teacher. You may want to get more practice using the resources at http://GalaxyGrammarBooks.com/Nebula for spelling. Your teacher can ask you other questions like the ones you missed and if you get them correct, you'll have earned your Spelling star and can move on to an adventure in grammar.

Unit IV: Adventures in Grammar

OFFICIAL GUARDIAN MAIL

Mission 20: Nouns

Dear fellow guardians,

We hope you have not disappeared and are able to read this letter. As you probably know, people, places, and things have been disappearing. What you may not know is who is responsible.

Remember General Arnold who caused problems with our phonics? He ordered our ships to remove nouns from Noun Town without permission. We are happy to report that those words have been returned. But the bad news is that we need your help to make sure only nouns have been returned. We also need to determine which street each word lived on.

Thank you in advance for your help. We are hoping our dear dog, Comet, will come back to us if we succeed. Please let us know if you see General Arnold anywhere!

Sincerely,

Kirk, Luke, and Ellen English

Guardians of Grammar Galaxy

P.S. You have been reviewing the words in your word book, haven't you? We sure don't need another vocabulary crisis!

☆ Step 1: On Guard & Put the Words That Are Not Nouns Back

On Guard. *Highlight TRUE or FALSE for each statement.*

1. Abbreviations and contractions are both short forms of words.	TRUE	FALSE
2. Swimmingpool is a correct compound word.	TRUE	FALSE
3. The word war comes before *word* in the dictionary.	TRUE	FALSE
4. A thesaurus gives synonyms for words.	TRUE	FALSE
5. You will probably read more if you read at the same time each day.	TRUE	FALSE

Say each of these words in a sentence. *Their meanings are given.*

pandemonium – *chaos* **apprehension** – *fear* **essential** – *necessary*

Put the words that are NOT nouns back on the spaceship. *Draw a line from the words that are NOT nouns to the spaceship.* ***Hint:*** *<u>Draw a line from words that are NOT people, places, or things</u>.*

book

cat

mom

ran

old

☆ Step 2: Sort Words by People, Places, and Things

Draw a line from each noun to the street where it lives.

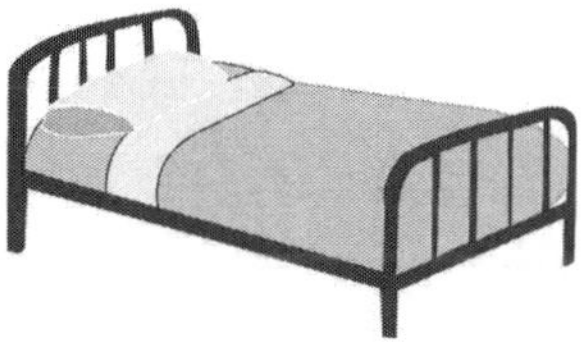

Activity. *Have your teacher write different kinds of nouns on small sticky notes and put them around the room(s) when you aren't looking. Go on a hunt to find them all. When you do, stick them in the right column for person, place, or thing.*

PERSON	PLACE	THING

☆ Step 3: Find Nouns in Sentences

Highlight nouns in the following sentences. *These are words that live in Noun Town because they are people, places, or things.*

1. The man and dog were friends.

2. The woman went into the bank.

3. The driver had a fast car.

4. The ship sailed near Africa.

5. The squirrel ate some nuts.

Vocabulary Victory! *Do you remember what these words mean? Check Step 1 if you forgot.*

pandemonium **apprehension** **essential**

☆ Advanced Guardians Only

Write or dictate a sentence using a person noun, place noun, and thing noun. *Your sentence will have at least three nouns.*

OFFICIAL GUARDIAN MAIL

Mission 20: Update

Dear guardians,

We are so happy to tell you that Comet is back home! We actually found the words *dog* and *pet* and brought them back to Thing Street personally. The museum, shopping mall, and stadium are all back too.

We wish we could tell you that General Arnold was in jail where he belongs, but we still haven't found him. We will have to stay alert to any nouns that are out of place.

We are attaching the solutions to this mission. Thank you for doing what you do to protect the galaxy!

Sincerely,

Kirk, Luke, and Ellen English

Guardians of Grammar Galaxy

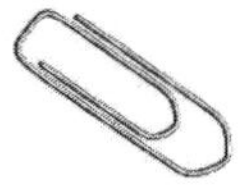

Step 1 Solutions

1.	Abbreviations and contractions are both short forms of words.	**TRUE**	FALSE
2.	Swimmingpool is a correct compound word.	TRUE	**FALSE**
3.	The word war comes before *word* in the dictionary.	**TRUE**	FALSE
4.	A thesaurus gives synonyms for words.	**TRUE**	FALSE
5.	You will probably read more if you read at the same time each day.	**TRUE**	FALSE

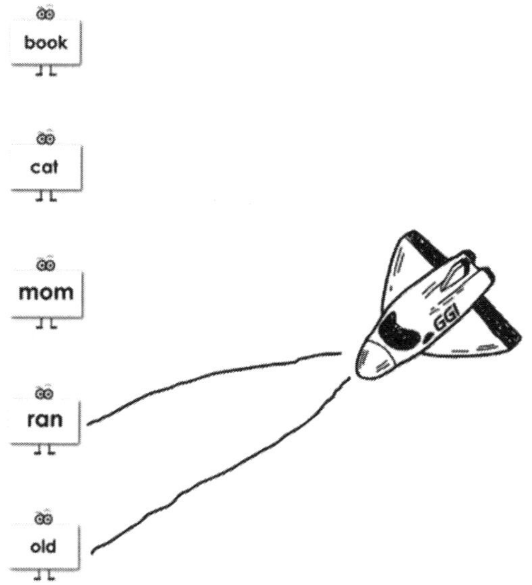

Step 2 Solutions

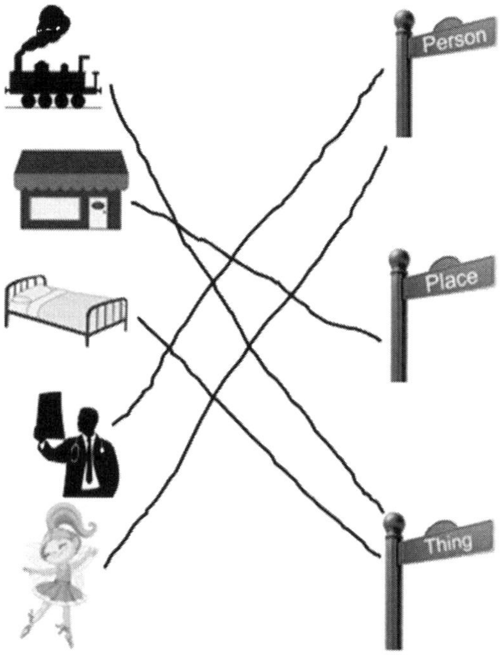

Step 3 Solutions:

1. The man and dog were friends.
2. The woman went into the bank.
3. The driver had a fast car.
4. The ship sailed near Africa.
5. The squirrel ate some nuts.

OFFICIAL GUARDIAN MAIL

Mission 21: Common and Proper Nouns

Dear guardians,

We hate to give you a mission in the middle of the Book Awards, but it's truly an emergency. The capital city received a threatening letter and as a result, the proper nouns living there have left. Now we aren't able to use proper nouns, even for the Book Awards. The good news is the capital is safe. Most likely the Gremlin or General Arnold sent the letter just to cause chaos. Unfortunately, the letter worked!

We are going to send Grammar Patrol out to look for proper nouns and transport them back to the capital. But we need to tell them which nouns are proper nouns. Can you help so the award ceremony can continue?

Your fellow guardians

P.S. We can't sign our names until the proper nouns are returned!

☆ Step 1: On Guard & Choose the Picture Described by a Proper Noun

On Guard. *Highlight the correct answer for each statement.*

1. Which word is a noun?
   guardian　　　goes

2. Nouns are people, places, and ________:
   actions　　　things

3. The abbreviation for Mister is:
   Mstr.　　　Mr.

4. What two words are the contraction won't short for?
   will not　　　why not

5. Which word has three syllables?
   summer　　　afternoon

Say each of these words in a sentence. *Their meanings are given.*

prestigious – *respected*　　**redeemed** – *saved*　　**exquisitely**– *beautifully*

Choose the picture in each pair described by a proper noun. *Circle the picture that has a specific name and should be returned to the capital.* ***Hint:*** *Proper nouns start with capital letters.*

Grace of the Seas

cat

Happy Farm

woman

Civic Center

Dilong

☆ Step 2: Find Proper Nouns That Aren't Capitalized

Highlight the proper nouns that should be capitalized in each sentence. *Hint:* *Names, book titles, initials, and titles like Mr. are always capitalized.*

1. ellen had always wished for a pet cat.
2. kirk has a pet fish he calls loch ness or l. n. for short.
3. luke named comet after a fast, white comet in the sky.
4. comet goes to a vet named dr. katz.
5. dr. katz wrote the book *i love big dogs*.

Activity. *Describe a trip you took without using any proper nouns. Every time you slip and use a proper noun, start over.*

☆ Step 3: Answer Questions with Proper Nouns

Highlight the proper nouns. *All three of the answers to the following questions are correct, but only one answer is a capitalized proper noun. Highlight it.*

1. The English family's favorite pet is:
   Comet   a white dog   comet

2. Green Eggs and Ham was written by:
   an author   Dr. Seuss   dr. seuss

3. The English family lives in:
   a galaxy   grammar galaxy   Grammar Galaxy

4. The three English children are:
   kirk, luke, and ellen   guardians   Kirk, Luke, and Ellen

5. An enemy of the galaxy is:
   Prefix   prefix   suffix

Vocabulary Victory! *Do you remember what these words mean? Check Step 1 if you forgot.*

prestigious   **redeemed**   **exquisitely**

☆ Advanced Guardians Only

Answer the questions using proper nouns. *Write or dictate the answers. If you dictate, tell your teacher when to use a capital letter.*

My name is ______________________________.

One book I love is

______________________________.

I live in ______________________________.

OFFICIAL GUARDIAN MAIL

Mission 21: Update

Dear guardians,

Thank you so much! The Book Awards will be able to continue with the winning authors' names and titles announced.

Grammar Patrol tells us that they were able to return most of the proper nouns to the capital, but they have asked us to continue to assist them. Please continue to look for names of people, places, and things that should be capitalized.

For now, we are so happy to be able to sign our names and see who wins at the Book Awards! We are attaching the solutions to this mission.

Sincerely,

Kirk, Luke, and Ellen English

Guardians of Grammar Galaxy

P.S. Which books would you choose as award winners?

Step 1 Solutions

On Guard.

1. Which word is a noun?
   guardian goes
2. Nouns are people, places, and ________:
   actions things
3. The abbreviation for Mister is:
   Mstr. Mr.
4. What two words is the contraction won't short for?
   will not why not
5. Which word has three syllables?
   summer afternoon

Step 2 Solutions

1. ellen had always wished for a pet cat.
2. kirk has a pet fish he calls loch ness or l. n. for short.
3. luke named comet after a fast, white comet in the sky.
4. comet goes to a vet named dr. katz.
5. dr. katz wrote the book *i love big dogs*.

Step 3 Solutions:

1. The English family's favorite pet is:

Comet	a white dog	comet

2. Green Eggs and Ham was written by:

an author	Dr. Seuss	dr. seuss

3. The English family lives in:

a galaxy	grammar galaxy	Grammar Galaxy

4. The three English children are:

kirk, luke, and ellen	guardians	Kirk, Luke, and Ellen

5. An enemy of the galaxy is:

Prefix	prefix	suffix

OFFICIAL GUARDIAN MAIL

Mission 22: Singular and Plural Nouns

Dear guardian,

Unfortunately, we cannot use the plural form of that greeting because S is still missing. Her sister E-s still refuses to tell police where she has her. Until she does, we won't be able to form a plural noun automatically. We need your help to add **-s** to any word that needs it. Remember that a word that ends in **ch**, **sh**, **x**, and **s** adds **–es** to make a plural. If you forget, just remember E-s's song "Don't You Wish You Were a Rich Fox with a Dress Like Mine?" Each underlined word needs an **–es** to be plural when it's used as a noun.

Ellen is especially grateful for all your help. She is so upset about her favorite singer!

Sincerely,

Kirk, Luke, and Ellen English

Guardian of Grammar Galaxy

P.S. Do you notice anything wrong with our title under our signature? It's another problem that the missing S has caused.

☆ Step 1: On Guard & Add Correct Endings

On Guard. *Answer the questions for your teacher.*

1. What is the difference between a common and proper noun?
2. Give examples of person, place, and thing nouns.
3. Spell a new word you've learned for your teacher.
4. What is the abbreviation for the word Avenue?
5. How can you guess the meaning of a word in a sentence?

Say each of these words in a sentence. *Their meanings are given.*

chided – *scolded* **contrite** – *sorry* **consulted** – *discussed*

Add correct endings. *Highlight the ending for each picture needed to make it plural.*

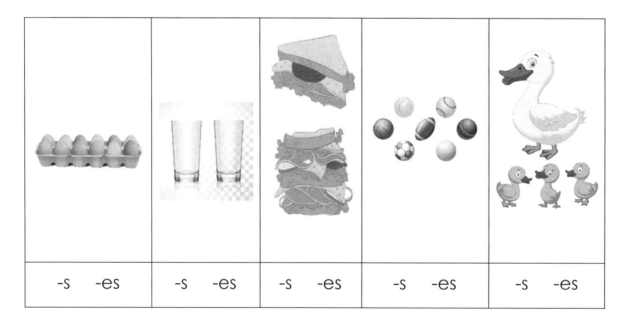

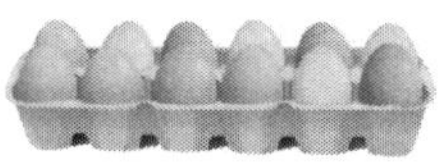		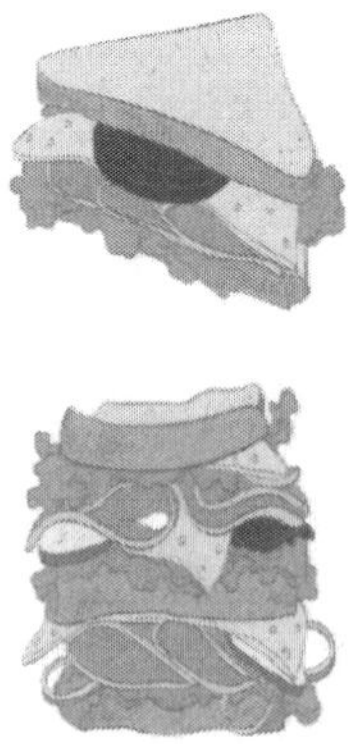	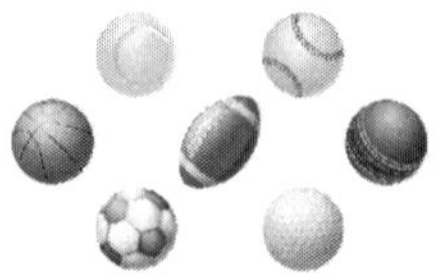	
-s -es	-s -es	-s -es	-s -es	-s -es

☆ Step 2: Find Plural Errors

Find the plural error in each sentence. *Highlight the word that is singular when it should be plural or that is an incorrect plural.*

1. Luke practices by hitting as many spaceball as he can.
2. Ellen listens to the Plural Sisters' songes over and over.
3. Comet loves to chase all the rabbit in the castle garden.
4. Kirk is reading about a genie who grants his owner three wishs.
5. The queen loves to collect watchs.

Activity. *Have your teacher find a box big enough to jump into. You can also use tape or string to create a box on the floor. Every time your teacher says a word that requires* **–es** *to make a plural like the word box, jump in it. If it requires an* **–s** *ending to make a plural instead, hiss like a snake. If it's already plural, don't do anything. Don't peek!*

Were you correct every time? **Teacher note**: *If your student can't jump, ask them about the words verbally.*

dish	pumpkin	shoes	jar	fox
rocks	flash	car	rich	cent
fire	toads	dash	fix	scoop

☆ Step 3: Add the Correct Plural Ending

Add –s or –es to each word to make it plural.

1. miss_____	2. word_____
3. book_____	4. ditch_____
5. noun_____	6. match_____

Vocabulary Victory! *Do you remember what these words mean? Check Step 1 if you forgot.*

chided **contrite** **consulted**

☆ Advanced Guardians Only

Write or dictate a fan letter to S. *Ellen thought it would be a great idea if we wrote S a letter to tell her we miss her and which song of hers we love most. Create a song title with as many plural words that end in* **–s** *that you can think of. When S is back, Ellen thinks she will love reading them. Be sure to sign your name!* ***Hint:*** *Each main word in a song title is capitalized.*

Official

S

Fan Mail

Dear S,

We miss you! My favorite song of yours is

"____

____

____

__________"

__________.

Your fan,

____

OFFICIAL GUARDIAN MAIL

Mission 22: Update

Dear guardians,

We have an update on S. Her sister E-s was so thrilled with all the publicity she was getting and the popularity of her lead song that she told police where she had put S. She apologized to S. Then when S started reading all the fan letters you sent her, she was so happy that she refused to press charges against her sister. The Plural Sisters will be going back on tour! A certain female member of our family is just a bit excited.

But to prevent this from being a problem in the future, we will ask you to practice making plurals every so often. We are attaching the solutions to this mission.

Sincerely,

Kirk, Luke, and English

Guardians of Grammar Galaxy

P.S. Did you notice we can write *Guardians* again?

<u>Step 1 Solutions</u>

On Guard.

1. **What is the difference between a common and proper noun?** A common noun names a general person, place, or thing while a proper noun gives the name of a specific person, place, or thing that is capitalized.
2. **Give examples of person, place, and thing nouns.** Answers will vary.
3. **Spell a new word you've learned for your teacher.** Answers will vary.
4. **What is the abbreviation for the word <u>Avenue</u>?** Ave.
5. **How can you guess the meaning of a word in a sentence?** Using the context or looking at the words and pictures around the unknown word.

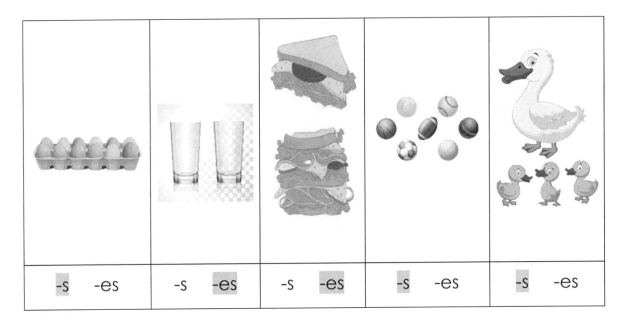

		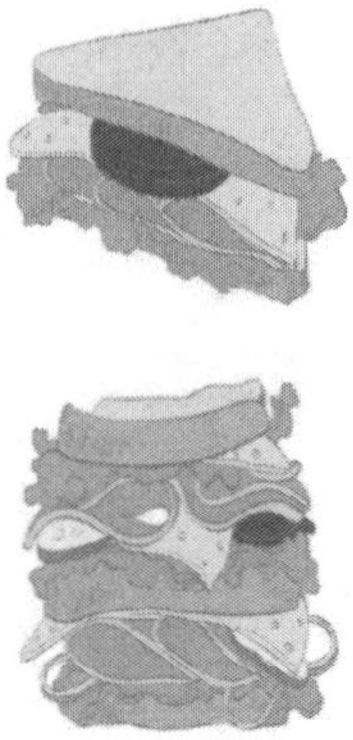	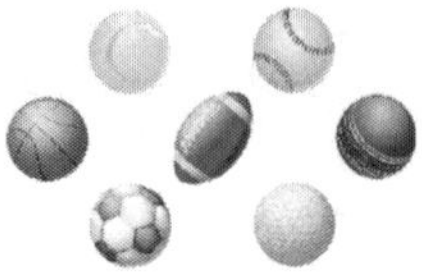	
-s -es	-s -es	-s -es	-s -es	-s -es

Step 2 Solutions

1. Luke practices by hitting as many spaceball as he can.
2. Ellen listens to the Plural Sisters' songes over and over.
3. Comet loves to chase all the rabbit in the castle garden.
4. Kirk is reading about a genie who grants his owner three wishs.
5. The queen loves to collect watchs.

Activity.

dish(box) pumpkin(hiss)	shoes	jar(hiss)	fox(box)
rocks	flash(box)	car(hiss)	rich(box) cent(hiss)
fire(hiss) toads	dash(box)	fix(box)	scoop(hiss)

Step 3 Solutions:

1. misses	2. words
3. books	4. ditches
5. nouns	6. matches

....

OFFICIAL GUARDIAN MAIL

Mission 23: Pronouns

Dear guardians,

The pronouns are gone and need help to get back home. If Kirk, Luke, and Ellen are exhausted from not being able to use them, the guardians probably are too. Please complete this mission as soon as possible!

Sincerely,

Kirk, Luke, and Ellen English

Guardians of Grammar Galaxy

☆ Step 1: On Guard & Choose the Correct Pronoun for Each Picture

On Guard. *Highlight TRUE or FALSE for each question.*

1. You don't need to know how to spell anymore. TRUE FALSE
2. Plural means more than one. TRUE FALSE
3. A proper noun is one that uses good manners. TRUE FALSE
4. A contraction uses a period. TRUE FALSE
5. A plot is found in a nonfiction book. TRUE FALSE

Say each of these words in a sentence. *Their meanings are given.*

consented – *agreed* **console** – *comfort* **accommodations** – *housing*

Choose the correct pronoun for each picture. *Highlight* ***he, she, it,*** *or* ***they***.

he she it they	he she it they	he she it they	he she it they	he she it they

☆ Step 2: Replace Words with Pronouns

Highlight the words that should replace the underlined word or words in the sentence. *Note:* *Pay attention to who is speaking*.

1. Ellen said, "Ellen wants to play Apples to Apples ®."

   I want　　　She wants

2. Luke said, "Kirk and Ellen are not playing fair."

   I am　　　You are

3. The king said, "The pronouns are not in Noun Town."

   They are　　　You are

4. The queen said, "The king, queen, and children need a snack."

   They need　　　We need

5. Luke said, "I don't want to play Apples to Apples ® anymore."

   them　　　it

Activity. *Describe what you did yesterday without using any pronouns. Can you do it?*

☆ Step 3: Write the Correct Pronoun

Write the pronoun I, me, he, him, she, her, it, we, or they to replace the underlined word or words. *Note:* *Pay attention to who is speaking.*

1. Ellen said, "Ellen love Comet." ______

2. Luke said, "I love Comet more." ______

3. Kirk said, "Don't forget Kirk!" ______

4. The king said, "The kids love Comet." ______

5. The queen said, "The king and queen do too." ______

Vocabulary Victory! *Do you remember what these words mean? Check Step 1 if you forgot.*

consented **console** **accommodations**

☆ Advanced Guardians Only

Add the correct pronouns to this letter to the pronouns which we hope will convince them to come home. ***Note:*** *Add the pronouns **we** or **you**. Remember to sign the letter!*

Official **Pronoun Fan Club** *Mail*

****

Dear Pronouns,

________ need ________! Please come home to Noun

Town. If ________ come home, ________ will name a street

after ________. ________ will also have a party for

________.

Sincerely,

____

OFFICIAL GUARDIAN MAIL

Mission 23: Update

Dear guardians,

You are the best! We are so happy that the pronouns are back safe and sound in Noun Town. We delivered your letters to them and they worked! The pronouns wanted to come home after Grammar Patrol let them out.

Plans are underway for a street dedication party in honor of the pronouns! Until then, check the answers to the mission we are attaching

Sincerely Yours,

Kirk, Luke, and Ellen English

Guardians of Grammar Galaxy

P.S. *Yours* is another kind of pronoun we learned about. Keep your eyes open for any pronouns that didn't go home!

Step 1 Solutions

On Guard.

1. You don't need to know how to spell anymore. TRUE **FALSE**
2. Plural means more than one. **TRUE** FALSE
3. A proper noun is one that uses good manners. TRUE **FALSE**
4. A contraction uses a period. TRUE **FALSE**
5. A plot is found in a nonfiction book. TRUE **FALSE**

he she it they	he she it they	he she it they	he she it they	he she it they

Note: **he** would also be acceptable for the gingerbread cookie.

Step 2 Solutions

1. Ellen said, "Ellen wants to play Apples to Apples."
   I want   She wants
2. Luke said, "Kirk and Ellen are not playing fair."
   I am   You are
3. The king said, "The pronouns are not in Noun Town."
   They are   You are
4. The queen said, "The king, queen, and children need a snack."
   They need   We need
5. Luke said, "I don't want to play Apples to Apples anymore."
   them   it

Step 3 Solutions:

1. Ellen said, "Ellen love Comet."   I
2. Luke said, "I love Comet more."   him
3. Kirk said, "Don't forget Kirk!"   me
4. The king said, "The kids love Comet."   They
5. The queen said, "The king and queen do too."   We

Advanced Guardians.

Dear Pronouns,

We need you! Please come home to Noun Town. If you come home, we will name a street after you. We will also have a party for you.

OFFICIAL GUARDIAN MAIL

Mission 24: Articles

Dear friends,

We are having an terrible time using the correct article ever since the Miss Article contest that was held on planet Sentence. Kirk has an idea for how to fix it, but can you give us an helping hand and tell us which words belong with the articles *a* and *an*? We would so appreciate it. We apologize for using the wrong article in this letter!

Sincerely,

Kirk, Luke, and Ellen English

Guardians of Grammar Galaxy

P.S. Can you tell where we used <u>an</u> incorrectly in this letter?

☆ Step 1: On Guard & Articles for Pictures

On Guard. *Highlight the correct answer for each question.*

1. Which is the plural form of the word match?
   match matchs matches

2. Which of these is a common noun?
   tiger Tiger Tigger

3. What kind of noun is nurse?
   person place thing

4. The word remake has a:
   prefix suffix

5. Which word comes before rock in the dictionary?
   rope rice rod

Say each of these words in a sentence. *Their meanings are given.*

glumly – *unhappily* **agitated** – *tense* **coincidence** – *accident*

Articles for pictures. *Draw a line from the picture to the correct article.* ***Hint:*** *Use the name for the kind of bird.*

☆ Step 2: Choose Articles for Words

Highlight *a* or *an* for each word.

ant	baby	hose	egg	inch
a an	a an	a an	a an	a an

Activity. *Which article do you think goes with the most words? Take a guess, then ask your teacher to count how many words you can think of to describe a book for a and an. Which article won?*

A________________book Number of words:______

An________________book Number of words:______

☆ Step 3: Highlight the Incorrect Articles

Highlight a or an if it isn't being used with the right word in each sentence. *Do nothing if the article is correct.*

1. Luke was sad that he did not catch a turtle.
2. He hoped to catch it with an net.
3. He would have kept it for an pet.
4. He needed a tank to keep it in.
5. But he was glad he got to take an trip instead.

Vocabulary Victory! *Do you remember what these words mean? Check Step 1 if you forgot.*

glumly **agitated** **coincidence**

☆ Advanced Guardians Only

Rewrite the sentence changing the underlined words to make it correct. *Get help spelling if you need it.*

I want to be a amazing reader so I can be a astronaut.

OFFICIAL GUARDIAN MAIL

Mission 24: Update

Dear friends,

You are an amazing group of guardians! Did you notice that *an* is the correct article for that compliment?

We are pleased to report that we threw an incredible party for A-list words who forgot all about *an* winning the Miss Article contest. Any word that was anybody was there! In fact, the party was so popular that some of the *an* fans tried to get in. A few may have gotten by us, so we will have to ask you to keep your article skills sharp in the future.

We are attaching the mission solutions.

Gratefully,

Kirk, Luke, and Ellen English

Guardians of Grammar Galaxy

Step 1 Solutions

On Guard.

1. Which is the plural form of the word match?
   match   matchs   **matches**
2. Which of these is a common noun?
   tiger   Tiger   Tigger
3. What kind of noun is nurse?
   person   place   thing
4. The word remake has a:
   prefix   suffix
5. Which word comes before rock in the dictionary?
   rope   **rice**   rod

Articles for pictures.

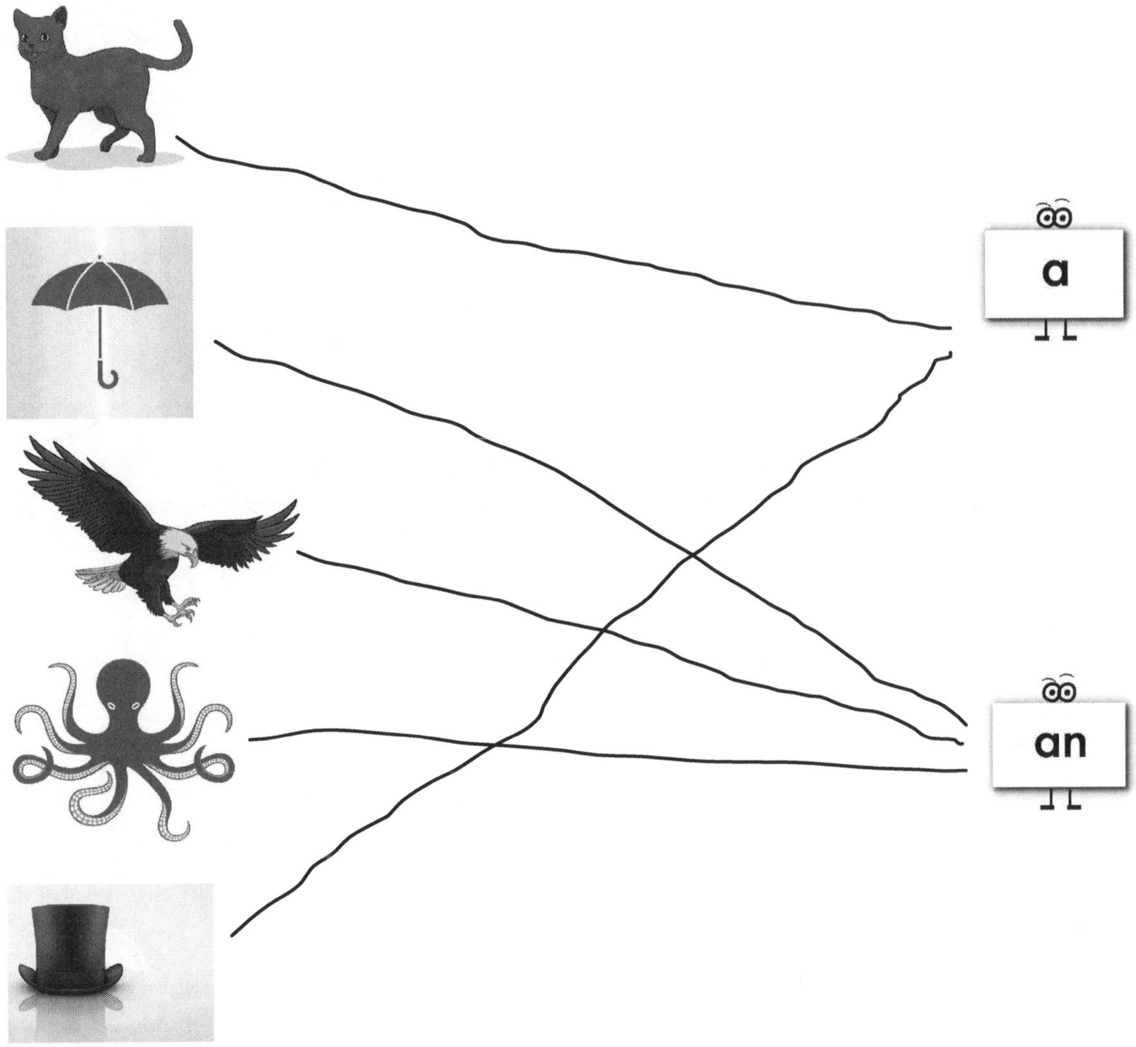

Step 2 Solutions

ant	baby	hose	egg	inch
a an	a an	a an	a an	a an

Step 3 Solutions:

1. Luke was sad that he did not catch a turtle.
2. He hoped to catch it with an net.
3. He would have kept it for an pet.
4. He needed a tank to keep it in.
5. But he was glad he got to take an trip instead.

OFFICIAL GUARDIAN MAIL

Mission 25: Adjectives

Dear guardians,

The adjectives on planet Sentence have gotten lost. We are on our way to help them get back home, but we will need your help to identify them. Luke hopes to get his communicator out of the library's Lost and Found if we succeed. Thanks in advance!

Sincerely,

Kirk, Luke, and Ellen English

Guardians of Grammar Galaxy

☆ Step 1: On Guard & Choose Adjectives for Pictures

On Guard. *Highlight the correct answer for each question.*

1. Which of the following words is a pronoun?
   Ellen Kirk me

2. Which word is a correct plural?
   sock socks sockes

3. Which word is a proper noun?
   Ellen sister her

4. Which word is a noun?
   fast go car

5. Which word is a correct compound word?
   didn't didnot sunroom

Say each of these words in a sentence. *Their meanings are given.*

complied – *obeyed* **resume** – *continue* **vague** – *unclear*

Choose adjectives for pictures. *For each picture, highlight the word that is an adjective that describes it.* ***Hint:*** *An adjective tells you which one, what kind, or how many and is not an action.*

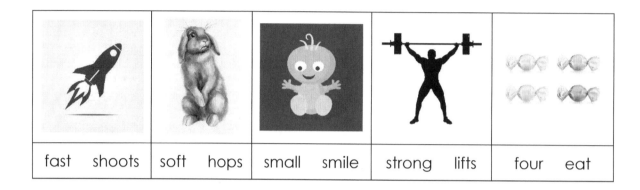

				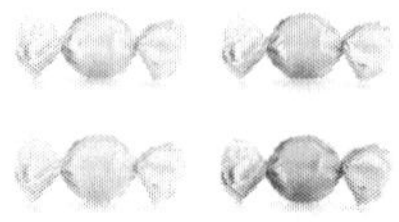
fast shoots	soft hops	small smile	strong lifts	four eat

☆ Step 2: Find the Adjectives in Sentences

Highlight the adjectives. *Adjectives often come right before nouns in sentences and tell you which one, what kind, or how many. The number in parentheses at the end of the sentences tells you how many adjectives you should highlight.*

1. Ellen likes to read in the beautiful garden. (1)

2. The queen likes to read for two long hours before bed. (2)

3. The king is a fast reader. (1)

4. Luke likes to read four funny books a week. (2)

5. Kirk likes to read three short mystery books a week. (3)

Activity. *Go on an adjectives scavenger hunt. The hunt can be done inside or out. Put an object in a bag for each adjective and check them off when you find them. Have your teacher make a copy of the list on the next page so you can have a competition. You can also time how long it takes you if you are hunting alone. When you're finished, show your teacher what you chose for each adjective.*

Adjective Scavenger Hunt

Find something:

- ☐ Round
- ☐ Green
- ☐ Smooth
- ☐ Rough
- ☐ Small
- ☐ Brown
- ☐ Dry
- ☐ Hard
- ☐ Three (find 3 of something)
- ☐ Pretty

☆ Step 3: Create with Adjectives

Draw what is described. *Draw what is described by each adjective and noun pair in the box on the right.*

one stick man	
a red apple	
five small dots	
a round, sliced pizza	
a happy face	

Vocabulary Victory! *Do you remember what these words mean? Check Step 1 if you forgot.*

complied **resume** **vague**

☆ Advanced Guardians Only

Write or dictate a sentence using adjectives to describe a friend.
Hint: *What kind of friend is s/he? How old is s/he? What does s/he look like?*

OFFICIAL GUARDIAN MAIL

Mission 25: Update

Dear trusted, hard-working guardians,

The adjectives are back! We found them and with your help, we knew right away who they were. We asked them questions like *which one*, *what kind*, and *how many* to be sure.

Now that we're able to use them again, Luke is going to go get his communicator. By the way, it's silver and rectangular. It has rounded edges and two black oval buttons on the side. That's a bunch of adjectives!

We are attaching the solutions to this mission.

Sincerely,

Kirk, Luke, and Ellen English

Guardians of Grammar Galaxy

Step 1 Solutions

On Guard.

1. Which of the following words is a pronoun?
   Ellen Kirk me
2. Which word is a correct plural?
   sock socks sockes
3. Which word is a proper noun?
   Ellen sister her
4. Which word is a noun?
   fast go car
5. Which word is a correct compound word?
   didn't didnot sunroom

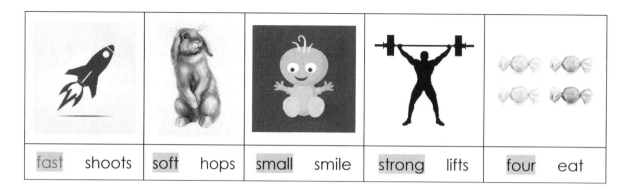

				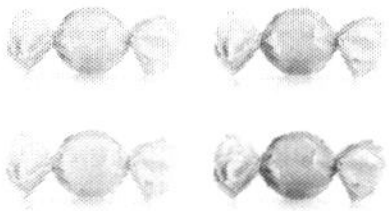
fast shoots	soft hops	small smile	strong lifts	four eat

Step 2 Solutions

1. Ellen likes to read in the beautiful garden. (1)
2. The queen likes to read for two long hours before bed. (2)
3. The king is a fast reader. (1)
4. Luke likes to read four funny books a week. (2)
5. Kirk likes to read three short mystery books a week. (3)

....

OFFICIAL GUARDIAN MAIL

Mission 26: Verbs

Dear guardians,

We hope you have more energy than we do because we have a very important mission for you. Most of the action verbs in the galaxy are sleeping at the Action Film Festival. This means it is difficult for us to do much of anything. We have to wake them up!

Our plan is to show a really popular action film at the festival. The problem is we will be charged per ticket for the movie. To keep costs down, we need you to tell us which words are action verbs so we can limit admission to them. We are on our way to the festival, so we hope you complete this mission as soon as you can.

Thanks in advance for your help.

Sincerely,

Kirk, Luke, and Ellen English

Guardians of Grammar Galaxy

☆ Step 1: On Guard & Find Action Verbs

On Guard. *Answer the following questions for your teacher.*

1. What are words that describe nouns called?

2. What are the three article adjectives?

3. What are nouns that take the place of other nouns to avoid repetition called?

4. What is a plural noun?

5. What is a prefix you learned and what does it mean?

Say each of these words in a sentence. *Their meanings are given.*

perturbed – *annoyed* **delectable** – *delicious* **stupor** – *daze*

Find action verbs. *Circle pictures that show actions*. ***Hint:*** *Sleeping is an action verb!*

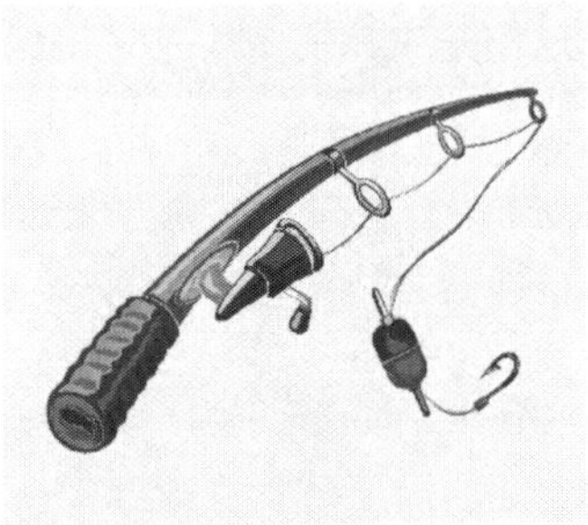

☆ Step 2: Find Verbs in Sentences

Highlight verbs. *Highlight the verb in each sentence.*

1. The English family rode to the gardens.

2. Comet slept in the castle.

3. The kids sat on benches.

4. The king ate his lunch.

5. The king complained.

Activity. *Roll a die and do the action corresponding to the number you roll. Play with your teacher, a sibling, or friend and see who gets the farthest away after four rolls each.* ***Hint:*** *Do nothing for* ***is*** *and* ***be****. Do you prefer to roll an action verb or state of being verb?*

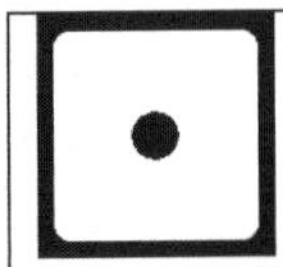	is
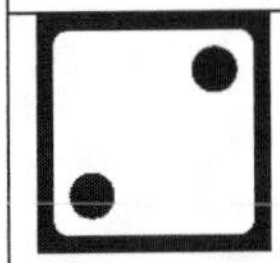	2 little hops
	3 skips
	be
	5 giant steps
	roll again

☆ Step 3: Add Verbs to Sentences

Highlight the action verb that should go in each sentence.

1. The kids __________ in the garden.
   were   are   walked

2. Comet __________ in the dining room.
   slept   was   is

3. Clouds __________ in the sky.
   were   moved   are

4. The family did not __________ lunch.
   their   yummy   eat

5. The family __________ home.
   went   is   are

Vocabulary Victory! *Do you remember what these words mean? Check Step 1 if you forgot.*

perturbed   **delectable**   **stupor**

☆ Advanced Guardians Only

Write what action movie you would show at the festival and which action verbs would love it most. *Remember to capitalize the movie title.*

I would show the movie ______________________________

____

and the action verbs that would love it most are: ______________

____

______________________________.

OFFICIAL GUARDIAN MAIL

Mission 26: Update

Dear guardians,

We are back from the Action Film Festival and the movie worked! We let the action verbs in and they stayed awake the whole time. They have gone back to Verb Village and we feel back to normal. We hope you do too. We've included the solutions to this mission.

Sincerely,

Kirk, Luke, and Ellen English

Guardians of Grammar Galaxy

Step 1 Solutions

On Guard.

1.**What are words that describe nouns called?** Adjectives.

2. **What are the three article adjectives?** a, an, the.

3. **What are nouns that take the place of other nouns to avoid repetition called?** Pronouns.

4. **What is a plural noun?** A noun that means more than one.

5. **What is a prefix you learned and what does it mean?** re- (do again) or un- (not or reverse).

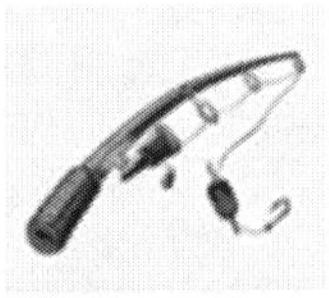

Step 2 Solutions

1. The English family rode to the gardens.
2. Comet slept in the castle
3. The kids sat on benches.
4. The king ate his lunch.
5. The king complained.

Step 3 Solutions:

1. The kids _________ in the garden.
   were are walked
2. Comet _________ in the dining room.
   slept was is
3. Clouds _________ in the sky.
   were moved are
4. The family did not _________ lunch.
   their yummy eat
5. The family _________ home.
   went is are

OFFICIAL GUARDIAN MAIL

Mission 27: Adverbs

Dear helpful guardians,

A painting has been stolen from the royal art gallery. We won't be able to solve the mystery until the adverbs have been returned to their original home near Verb Village.

Your mission, if you choose to accept it, is to help us identify adverbs so we can get them home. If we succeed, we should know when, where, and how the theft happened.

With gratitude,

Luke and Ellen English

Guardians of Grammar Galaxy

P.S. We can't end with our usual closing. Do you know why?

☆ Step 1: On Guard & Choose Adverbs for Pictures

On Guard. *Highlight the correct answer for each question.*

1. Which of the following words is a verb?
   go hat food

2. Which of the following words is an adjective?
   fun go food

3. Which of the following words is a pronoun?
   I Ellen girl

4. Which of the following words is singular?
   boy girls children

5. Which of the following words is spelled correctly?
   went wunt wint

Say each of these words in a sentence. *Their meanings are given.*

bespectacled – *glasses-wearing* **observation** – *watching* **grimacing** – *frowning*

Choose adverbs for pictures. *For each picture, highlight the word that is an adverb that describes it.* ***Note****: <u>An adverb tells you when, where, or how</u>.*

clock now	slowly turtle	fold neatly	point there	quickly run

☆ Step 2: Find the Adverbs in Sentences

Highlight the adverbs. *Adverbs often come right before or after verbs in the sentence. The action verb is underlined for you. Highlight the adverb that tells how, when, or where. The number in parentheses tells you how many adverbs there are.*

1. Kirk's head hit hard on the floor. (1)

2. The thief quickly ran away. (2)

3. The queen walked here fast. (2)

4. The detective returns tomorrow. (1)

5. The adverbs move slowly there now. (3)

Activity. *Play adverb charades. See if your teacher, family, or friends can guess the adverb you are acting out. Before you begin, look up any adverbs you don't know in the dictionary. Have your teacher help you if you need it. Roll two dice and act out the verb you roll for one die and the adverb you roll for the other. For example, if you rolled a 1 for both, you would climb suspiciously.*

	Verb	Adverb
	climb	suspiciously
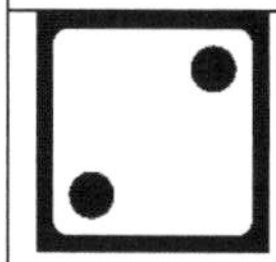	eat	carelessly
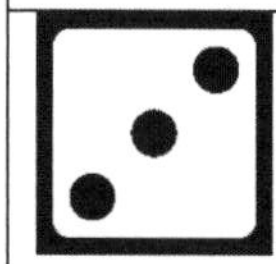	fall	angrily
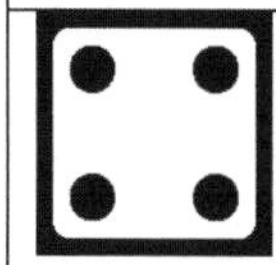	search	gracefully
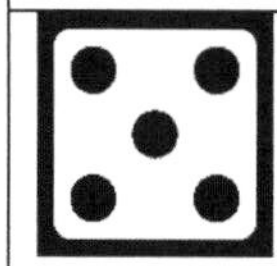	shake	nervously
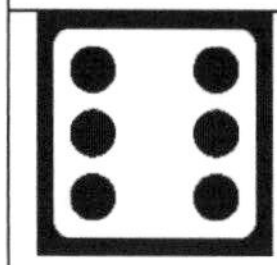	wash	sleepily

☆ Step 3: Choose Adverbs

Highlight the missing adverb. *For each sentence, highlight the adverb that is missing.*

1. Kirk saw the thief __________ at night.

   happy late eat

2. He was hiding __________ in the gallery.

   food art there

3. He stood __________ at first.

   run quietly dark

4. __________ he charged.

   Kirk art Later

5. He __________ escaped.

   quickly did will

Vocabulary Victory! *Do you remember what these words mean? Check Step 1 if you forgot.*

bespectacled **observation** **grimacing**

☆ Advanced Guardians Only

Write adverbs to complete the description of how the thief got away with the painting.

The thief was ______________________ hiding in the art

gallery and ______________________ ran

______________________ when the lights came on.

OFFICIAL GUARDIAN MAIL

Mission 27: Update

Dear friends,

With your help, we have been able to move most of the adverbs back to their home near Verb Village. As a result, Kirk has been able to answer the detective's questions about the crime. I (Kirk) am feeling better. The castle staff was also able to answer questions and we know our night watchman didn't steal the painting. He did admit, however, that he was sleeping when the thief ran out of the gallery. We still don't know exactly who the thief was or how he got in, but we suspect the Gremlin had something to do with it. The investigation is ongoing.

Sincerely,

Kirk, Luke, and Ellen English

Guardians of Grammar Galaxy

Step 1 Solutions

On Guard.

1. Which of the following words is a verb?
   go hat food
2. Which of the following words is an adjective?
   fun go food
3. Which of the following words is a pronoun?
   I Ellen girl
4. Which of the following words is singular?
   boy girls children
5. Which of the following words is spelled correctly?
   went wunt wint

clock now	slowly turtle	fold neatly	point there	quickly run

Step 2 Solutions

1. Kirk's head hit hard on the floor. (1)
2. The thief quickly ran away. (2)
3. The queen walked here fast. (2)
4. The detective returns tomorrow. (1)
5. The adverbs move slowly there now. (3)

Step 3 Solutions:

1. Kirk saw the thief _________ at night.
   happy late eat
2. He was hiding _________ in the gallery.
   food art there
3. He stood _________ at first.
   run quietly dark
4. _________ he charged.
   Kirk art Later
5. He _________ escaped.
   quickly did will

OFFICIAL GUARDIAN MAIL

Mission 28: End Marks

Dear guardians!

Forgive us if our end marks are incorrect? They have been removed and mixed up on planet Sentence and we have to do something?

Please complete this mission so we can put the periods, question marks, and exclamation points back where they belong? Remember that periods go with declarative sentences, question marks with interrogative sentences, and exclamation points with exclamatory sentences?

Sincerely!

Kirk, Luke, and Ellen English

Guardians of Grammar Galaxy

☆ Step 1: On Guard & Choose End Marks for Pictures

On Guard. *Highlight TRUE or FALSE for each statement.*

1. Adverbs tell more about nouns. TRUE FALSE

2. Verbs are people, places, or things. TRUE FALSE

3. Adjectives describe nouns. TRUE FALSE

4. Pronouns describe nouns. TRUE FALSE

5. The Plural Sisters are S, E-s, and Irregular. TRUE FALSE

Say each of these words in a sentence. *Their meanings are given.*

fatigued – *tired* **legislators** – *lawmakers* **petrified** – *terrified*

Choose end marks for pictures. *Draw a line from each picture/sentence to the end mark that should go with it.*

The house is on fire

It's a sunny day

Ouch

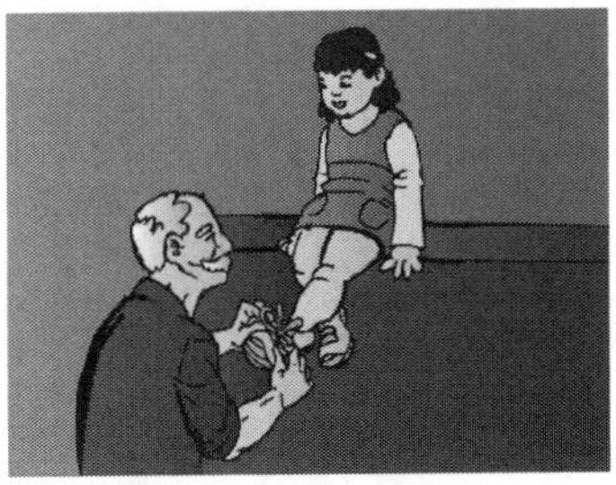

Will you help me

Why do we have to go

☆ Step 2: Choose Sentence Types

Highlight the sentence type. *Declarative sentences are statements that end in periods (.). Interrogative sentences are questions ending in a question mark (?). Exclamatory sentences express strong emotion and end in an exclamation mark (!).*

1. What is it

   declarative interrogative exclamatory

2. Oh no

   declarative interrogative exclamatory

3. I want to go to the zoo

   declarative interrogative exclamatory

4. Why are you shouting

   declarative interrogative exclamatory

5. Come on

   declarative interrogative exclamatory

Activity. *Have your teacher read the following sentences to you.* ***Don't peek!*** *For each sentence, stand still if it should end with a period, jump straight up and down if it should end with an exclamation mark, or put your arms to your side with palms up as though you're asking why for a question mark. Did you do them correctly?*

1. When can we have lunch?
2. We have to leave right now!
3. I want you to sit down.
4. Did you get all those?
5. Show me what to do for an interrogative sentence!

Teacher note: This should confuse your student, so discuss it.

☆ Step 3: Add the Missing End Mark

Add a period (.) question mark (?) or exclamation point (!) to the end of each sentence. *Get help reading the sentences if you need it.*

1. The king wanted to spend time with his family

2. Why didn't the kids ask to leave

3. Unbelievable

4. What is wrong

5. That is what Kirk wanted to know

Vocabulary Victory! *Do you remember what these words mean? Check Step 1 if you forgot.*

fatigued **legislators** **petrified**

☆ Advanced Guardians Only

Write I can't three times below with a period, question mark, and then an exclamation mark. *Then read them to see the difference an end mark can make.*

OFFICIAL GUARDIAN MAIL

Mission 28: Update

Dear guardian friends,

Whew! Because you finished the mission, we were able to get most of the end mark signs put back where they belong. We are not shouting when we don't mean to and we are all getting along better. Father ruled that the new beautification law doesn't apply to end mark signs.

How did the mission go for you? We are attaching the solutions to the mission.

Sincerely,

Kirk, Luke, and Ellen English

Guardians of Grammar Galaxy

Step 1 Solutions

On Guard.

1. Adverbs tell more about nouns. TRUE **FALSE**
2. Verbs are people, places, or things. TRUE **FALSE**
3. Adjectives describe nouns. **TRUE** FALSE
4. Pronouns describe nouns. TRUE **FALSE**
5. The Plural Sisters were S, E-s, and Irregular. **TRUE** FALSE

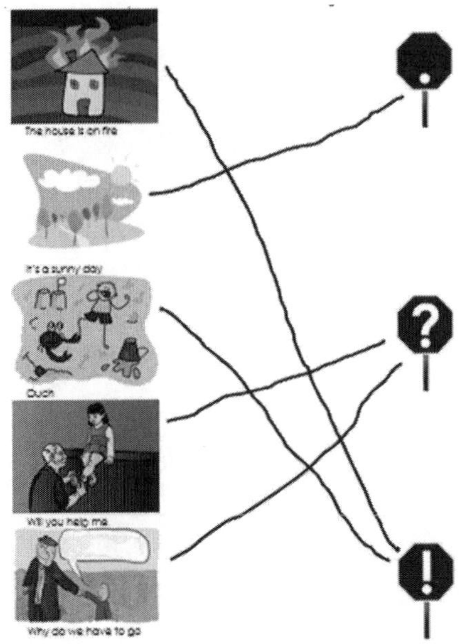

Step 2 Solutions

1. What is it

   declarative | interrogative | exclamatory

2. Oh no

   declarative | interrogative | exclamatory

3. I want to go to the zoo

   declarative | interrogative | exclamatory

4. Why are you shouting

   declarative | interrogative | exclamatory

5. Come on

   declarative | interrogative | exclamatory

Step 3 Solutions:

1. The king wanted to spend time with his family.
2. Why didn't the kids ask to leave?
3. Unbelievable!
4. What is wrong?
5. That is what Kirk wanted to know.

....

OFFICIAL GUARDIAN MAIL

Mission 29: Quotation Marks

Dear fellow guardians,

We hope you haven't read the article in today's *Grammar Gazette* about our father, the king. If you have, please know that the article had a number of untruths. We believe we know why. The article contains no direct quotes which would have made the king's statements clear.

We have learned that no direct quotes can be printed because the quotation marks on planet Sentence have been painted over. They are considered graffiti, even though we need them!

Your mission is to help us determine where quotation marks belong so we can put them back. Once we do, we hope the reporter will write a follow-up article giving direct quotes from the king that will share the truth.

Thank you so very much. We will report back soon.

Sincerely,

Kirk and Ellen English

Guardians of Grammar Galaxy

☆ Step 1: On Guard & Decide if Sentences Need Quotation Marks

On Guard. *Answer the questions for your teacher.*

1. What is an interrogative sentence?

2. What kind of word often ends in **–ly**?

3. A, an, and the are called what?

4. What is a proper noun?

5. What is vocabulary?

Say each of these words in a sentence. *Their meanings are given.*

monarch – *ruler* **fretfully** – *worriedly* **cringed** – *flinched*

Decide if sentences need quotation marks. *Circle the direct quotation sign if the sentence needs quotation marks or the indirect quotation blank sign if it does not.* ***Hint:*** *Sentences that need quotation marks often have a comma before or after what is said and the first word said is capitalized.*

1. The king said, I don't want people to think I am Superman.

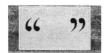

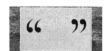

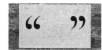

2. The king said he didn't want people to think he was Superman.

3. The king said, My biographer was too kind.

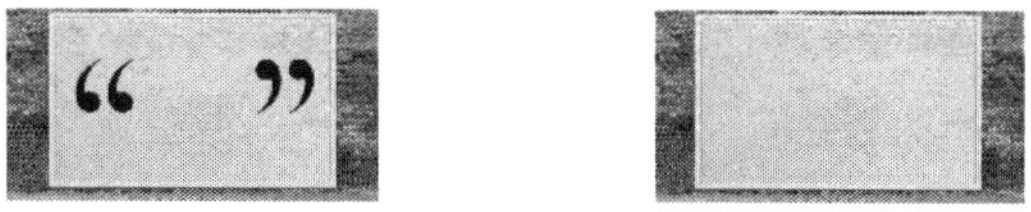

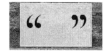

4. The king told the reporter that his biographer was too kind.

5. The police don't have a suspect yet, the king said.

☆ Step 2: Add Quotation Marks to Sentences

Add quotation marks. *Each sentence below needs quotation marks. Put them around what was said, including the quote's end mark or ending comma.*

1. Don't lose your temper,   the queen said.

2. This is terrible reporting!   the king yelled.

3. Poor Father,   Ellen said sadly.

4. Kirk said,   Let's look it up in the dictionary.

5. Ellen asked,   How do we fix it?

Activity. *Have your teacher make the following statements and then give a direct or indirect quote of it (as instructed) without peeking. For example, an indirect quote of "I am 36 years old" might be* You said you are 30-something*. A direct quote is* "I am 36 years old." You said, "I am 36 years old." *Listen carefully!*

1. I am hungry. (direct quote)
2. Reading is important because it builds spelling, vocabulary, grammar, and writing skills. (indirect quote)
3. I like to read for fun. (direct quote)
4. My favorite vacation spot is______. (direct quote)
5. One funny thing that happened to me as a kid is______. (indirect quote)

☆ Step 3: Add Missing Quotation Marks

Add quotation marks to the beginning and end of what the king actually said in this newspaper article. *Get help reading if needed. Make sure the end mark is inside the last set of quotation marks.*

I asked the king if what I had heard about the mistakes in his biography were true and he said, My biographer was too kind.

When I asked him more about it, he said, I want my biography to be rewritten. He also said, I don't want people to think I am Superman!

I also asked the king about the theft of a painting from the castle. He said, The police don't have a suspect yet. Finally, he told me, We are cooperating with them to solve the crime.

Vocabulary Victory! *Do you remember what these words mean? Check Step 1 if you forgot.*

monarch **fretfully** **cringed**

☆ Advanced Guardians Only

Interview your teacher. *Ask about his or her best traits and write it as a quote. For example*: My teacher said, "My best traits are ___, ___, and ___." *Get help spelling if you need it.*

OFFICIAL GUARDIAN MAIL

Mission 29: Update

Dear fellow guardians,

We are back home and are we ever tired! We were able to convince the painters who were painting over the quotation marks to add them back, but we still had to help. It was hard work, but without you telling us where the quotation marks belonged, it would have been impossible. Thank you so much. Father ruled that quotation marks aren't graffiti, but we might have missed some marks that were painted over. Be looking for them!

Were you able to complete the mission? We are attaching solutions as well as the Grammar Challenge. We know you can get at least 9 questions correct.

Sincerely,

Kirk, Luke, and Ellen English

Guardians of Grammar Galaxy

Step 1 Solutions

On Guard.

1. **What is an interrogative sentence?** An interrogative sentence asks a question and ends in a question mark.
2. **What kind of word often ends in –ly?** Adverbs.
3. **A, an, and the are called what?** Articles or article adjectives.
4. **What is a proper noun?** A noun that names a specific person, place, or thing that is capitalized.
5. **What is vocabulary?** All the words you know and use correctly.

Step 2 Solutions

1. "Don't lose your temper," the queen said.
2. This is terrible reporting!" the king yelled.
3. "Poor Father," Ellen said sadly.
4. Kirk said, "Let's look it up in the dictionary."

5. Ellen asked, "How do we fix it?"

Step 3 Solutions:

I asked the king if what I had heard about the mistakes in his biography were true and he said, "My biographer was too kind."

When I asked him more about it, he said, "I want my biography to be rewritten." He also said, "I don't want people to think I am Superman!"

I also asked the king about the theft of a painting from the castle. He said, "The police don't have a suspect yet." Finally, he told me, "We are cooperating with them to solve the crime."

Grammar Challenge I

***Carefully read or listen to all the possible answers** and then highlight the letter for the **<u>one</u> best answer**.*

1. **A noun is a:**
   a. person
   b. place
   c. person, place, or thing
2. **The following word is a proper noun:**
   a. pet
   b. dog
   c. Max
3. **The following word becomes plural by adding –es:**
   a. mother
   b. stick
   c. wish
4. **A pronoun is:**
   a. a noun that has turned pro
   b. a noun that takes the place of another noun
   c. a wise saying
5. **<u>An</u> is used before words that:**
   a. begin with vowel sounds
   b. begin with consonants
   c. begin with consonants or vowels
6. **Adjectives describe:**
   a. verbs
   b. nouns
   c. both verbs and nouns

7. The words as, am, and was are:

a. action verbs

b. state of being verbs

c. article adjectives

8. Words that end in –ly are usually:

a. nouns

b. verbs

c. adverbs

9. Periods are:

a. end marks

b. what follow a statement

c. both end marks and what follow a statement

10. Quotation marks are:

a. graffiti

b. used in direct quotes

c. used in indirect quotes

Number Correct:________/10

☆ *Extra Challenge*

How many of these vocabulary words can you remember the meaning of?

pandemonium	**apprehension**	**essential**	**prestigious**
redeemed	**exquisitely**	**chided**	**contrite**
consulted	**consented**	**console**	**accommodations**
glumly	**agitated**	**coincidence**	**complied**
resume	**vague**	**perturbed**	**delectable**
stupor	**bespectacled**	**observation**	**grimacing**
fatigued	**legislators**	**petrified**	**monarch**
fretfully	**cringed**		

Number Correct:________/30

Grammar Challenge 1 Answers

1.c; 2.c; 3.c; 4.b; 5.a; 6.b; 7.b; 8.c; 9.c; 10.b

If you got 9 or more correct, congratulations! You've earned your Grammar Star. You can color the star or add a sticker to your Grammar Guardian bookmark. You are ready for an adventure in composition.

If you did not get 9 or more correct, don't worry. You have another chance. You may want to have your teacher review the information from each chapter you've read so far. Then take the Grammar Challenge 2. Remember to **choose the one best answer**.

Extra Challenge Answers

Here are the meanings of the vocabulary words. Review, say them in a sentence, and see if you can remember more of them.

pandemonium - *chaos*	**apprehension** - *fear*	**essential** – *necessary*
prestigious – *respected*	**redeemed** - *saved*	**exquisitely** – *beautifully*
chided - *scolded*	**contrite** – *sorry*	**consulted** – *discussed*
consented - *agreed*	**console** - *comfort*	**accommodations** - *housing*
glumly - *unhappily*	**agitated** - *tense*	**coincidence** - *accident*
complied – *obeyed*	**resume** - *continue*	**vague** – *unclear*
perturbed - annoyed	**delectable** – *delicious*	**stupor** - *daze*
bespectacled – *glasses-wearing*	**observation** - *watching*	**grimacing** - *frowning*
fatigued - *tired*	**legislators** - *lawmakers*	**petrified** – *terrified*
monarch – ruler	**fretfully** - *worriedly*	**cringed** - *flinched*

Grammar Challenge 2

***Carefully read or listen to all the possible answers** and then highlight the letter for the **one best answer**.*

1. **Which word is a noun?**
   a. run
   b. runner
   c. fastest
2. **Proper nouns are always:**
   a. capitalized
   b. alphabetized
   c. short
3. **Which word is plural?**
   a. book
   b. game
   c. shoes
4. **Which word is a pronoun?**
   a. Susie
   b. I
   c. girl
5. **Which word could follow the article a?**
   a. sweet
   b. amazing
   c. ugly
6. **Which word is an adjective?**
   a. two
   b. big
   c. both *two* and *big*

7. Which word is a verb?

a. jump

b. fast

c. high

8. Which word is an adverb?

a. bed

b. now

c. big

9. This sentence should end with an exclamation point (!):

a. Can I go

b. I am seven

c. Help

10. Which sentence needs quotation marks?

a. He yelled, I'm here!

b. He told me he did not take it.

c. She said she wanted me to go.

Number Correct:________/10

Grammar Challenge 2 Answers

1.b; 2.a; 3.c; 4.b; 5.a; 6.c; 7.a; 8.b; 9.c; 10.a

If you got 9 or more correct, congratulations! You've earned your Grammar Star. You can color the star or add a sticker to your Grammar Guardian bookmark. You are now ready for an adventure in composition.

If you did not get 9 or more correct, don't worry. Review the questions you missed with your teacher. You may want to get more practice using the resources at http://GrammarGalaxyBooks.com/Nebula for grammar. Your teacher can ask you other questions like the ones you missed and if you get them correct, you'll have earned your Grammar star and can move on to an adventure in composition.

Unit V: Adventures in Composition & Speaking

OFFICIAL GUARDIAN MAIL

Mission 30: Handwriting

Dear guardians and fellow students,

No doubt you have noticed that your handwriting is very slow. I have learned that there is a lot of road construction in Handwriting City that explains the problem, but I have also spoken with the king. He explained that another reason our handwriting is slow is because we don't do it often enough. The less we write by hand, the slower we will write, making it harder to do some of our lessons.

I am giving you a mission to increase your handwriting speed. The good news is that the faster we write, the faster road construction will be completed. I know I can count on you!

Sincerely,

Kirk English

Guardian of Grammar Galaxy

☆ Step 1: On Guard & Practice Forming Each Letter

On Guard. *Highlight TRUE or FALSE for each question.*

1. Quotation marks are used for indirect quotes. TRUE FALSE
2. End marks are a, an, and the. TRUE FALSE
3. The word sun can be spelled correctly using phonics. TRUE FALSE
4. The word wonderful has a suffix. TRUE FALSE
5. Homographs like wind / wind always rhyme. TRUE FALSE

Say each of these words in a sentence. *Their meanings are given.*

gaped – *stared* **administrator** – *manager* **hastily** – *hurriedly*

Practice forming each letter. *Ask your teacher whether you should practice print, cursive, or manuscript. Follow the arrows in order. You may want to use a fine-point black marker.* ***Note***: *<u>You do NOT have to practice each handwriting style</u>.*

PRINT

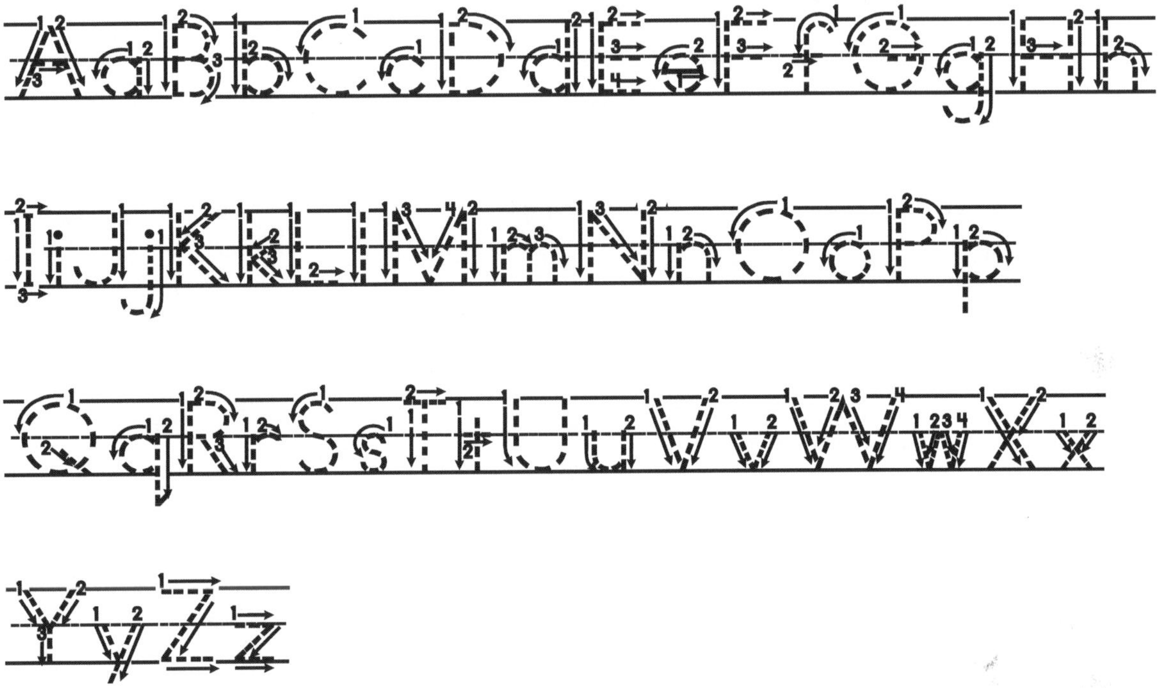

CURSIVE

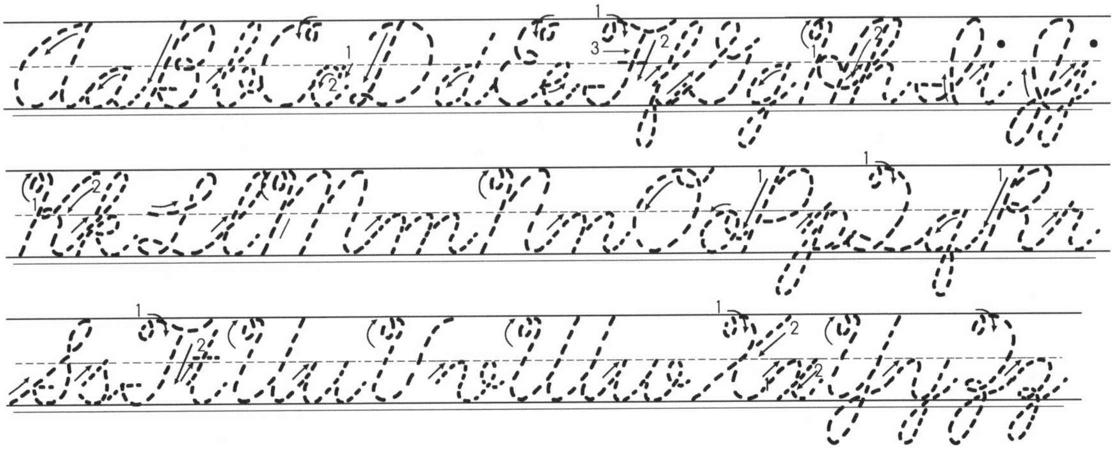

MANUSCRIPT

☆ Step 2: Practice from Memory

Review the alphabet and letters. *Write over the dotted letters, cover them, and write them from memory on the PRACTICE lines following.* ***Note:*** *Only do the handwriting style your teacher chose for you.*

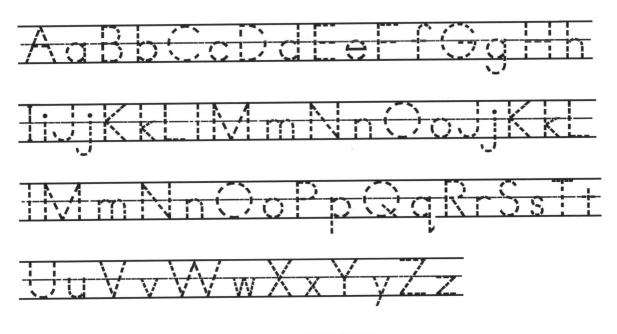

PRINT

Aa Bb Cc Dd Ee Ff Gg Hh

Ii Jj Kk Ll Mm Nn Oo Jj Kk Ll

Ll Mm Nn Oo Pp Qq Rr Ss Tt

Uu Vv Ww Xx Yy Zz

CURSIVE

Aa Bb Cc Dd Ee Ff Gg Hh Ii Jj

Kk Ll Mm Nn Oo Pp Qq Rr S

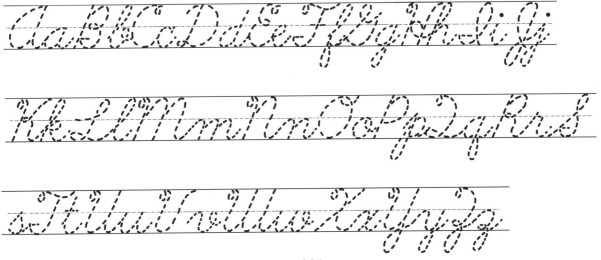

s Tt Uu Vv Ww Xx Yy Zz

MANUSCRIPT

AaBbCcDdEeFfGgHhIiJjKkLl

MmNnOoPpQqRrSsTtUuVvWw

XxYyZz

PRACTICE

☆ Step 3: Increase Handwriting Speed

Get a baseline and try to beat it. *Have your teacher time how many upper and lower case alphabet letters you can write in one minute. Then try to increase your speed in the next timed minute.* ***Note:*** *Letters should be formed correctly, but not perfectly.*

How many total letters (upper and lower case of a letter count as 2) did you write in one minute? ____________

Now try to beat that score in a second one-minute race on the next page.

Total letters written in 1 minute:

Date:

Vocabulary Victory! *Do you remember what these words mean? Check Step 1 if you forgot.*

gaped **administrator** **hastily**

☆ Advanced Guardians Only

Have a speed competition. *Your handwriting speed will increase as you get older. But you can have a competition with your teacher, a sibling, or friend who is a different age. See who can improve their speed the most over their baseline (or the first test taken). You can choose to see who wins two out of three tests. Have your teacher photocopy the next page, use handwriting paper of your choice, or download and print a form from http://GrammarGalaxyBooks.com/Nebula.*

Total letters written in 1 minute: ____________________

Baseline letters written in 1 minute: ____________________

Number of letters improved: ____________________

OFFICIAL GUARDIAN MAIL

Mission 30: Update

Dear guardians,

In the spirit of this mission, I decided to write this update by hand. I am happy to report that handwriting speeds have increased! Father has added more construction workers and our combined efforts have resulted in great progress.

However, it is very important for you to keep trying to increase your handwriting speed. It makes any kind of written work easier.

Sincerely Yours,

Kirk English

Guardian of Grammar Galaxy

Step 1 Solutions

On Guard.

1. Quotation marks are used for indirect quotes. TRUE **FALSE**
2. End marks are *a*, *an*, and *the*. TRUE **FALSE**
3. The word sun can be spelled correctly using phonics. **TRUE** FALSE
4. The word wonderful has a suffix. **TRUE** FALSE
5. Homographs like wind / wind always rhyme. TRUE **FALSE**

OFFICIAL GUARDIAN MAIL

Mission 31: Forms

Dear library card holders and friends,

When I tried to check out a book at the library, I was told I needed to complete a new library card application. Father is going to talk to the head librarian about allowing us to use the old application if none of our information has changed. But we still need to know how to fill out forms.

I am giving you a mission that will help you complete forms in the future. And now I am off to check out my book!

Sincerely,

Luke English

Guardian of Grammar Galaxy

☆ Step 1: On Guard & Complete a Reference Form

On Guard. *Highlight the correct answer for each question.*

1. The proper noun New York would live on which street?
   Person St. Place St. Thing St.

2. Which of these is a plural noun?
   running fines candy

3. Adjectives tell us:
   which one how where

4. Which word is spelled correctly?
   trusst trest trust

5. Writing by hand improves:
   spelling running typing

Say each of these words in a sentence. *Their meanings are given.*

dutifully – *obediently* **envisioned** – *imagined* **assistance** – *help*

Personal information form. *With your teacher's or parent's help, complete the form on the next page. Copy it and file it with other records or scan it and store it digitally. You can also print a form from http://GrammarGalaxyBooks.com/Nebula.*

My Personal Information

Full Name____

Month/Day/Year of Birth______/______/______ Age______ Gender: M or F (circle)

Street Address/Apt.#/P.O. Box________________________________

____

City_________________________ State__________ Zip Code__________

Primary phone number (   )________-________

Emergency phone number (   )________-________

Emergency Contact Name________________________________

Parents' or Guardians' Names________________________________

Parent Street Address (if different)____________________________

City_________________________ State__________ Zip Code__________

Parents'/Guardians' Email Addresses

Name______________________ Email________________________

Name______________________ Email________________________

Parents'/Guardians' Phone Numbers: Circle Home, Work, or Mobile

Name__________________________ (   )________-________ H W M

Name__________________________ (   )________-________ H W M

School____

Allergies?____

Other Medical Information________________________________

☆ Step 2: Complete a Library Card Application

Using the reference form you completed in Step 1, complete the practice library card application. *Sign your name!*

Student Library Card Application

First Name	Middle Name	Last Name
Street Address		Apt. #/P.O. Box
City	State	Zip Code
Phone Number ( ) -	Date of Birth – MM/DD/YY / /	Parent Email

Student Signature____

Activity. *Most public libraries allow students to have their own library card. Practice your form completion skills by filling out an application for a card the next time you go to the library.* ***Note:*** *Many libraries require proof of address and a parent's photo I.D.*

☆ Step 3: Complete Forms with Boxes

Use capital letters to complete a box form. *Leave a blank box between words. DOB stands for date of birth. If your birthdate has a day or month with only one digit (like Jan. 4, 2002 for 1/4/2), fill a 0 in before any single numbers like so:*

DOB – MM/DD/YY

0	1	0	4	0	2

LAST NAME

FIRST NAME

ADDRESS

DOB – MM/DD/YY

Vocabulary Victory! *Do you remember what these words mean? Check Step 1 if you forgot.*

dutifully **envisioned** **assistance**

☆ Advanced Guardians Only

Practice completing a Reading Buddy application to be a library volunteer. *Fill out the application on the next page. See if your library has a reading buddy program if you like!* ***Note****:* *Put an X next to male or female.*

Child name______________________________

Male____ **Female**____ **Age**____

Name of parent or guardian______________________________

Address______________________________

____

Phone______________ **Email**______________

School______________________________

Kinds of books you read______________________________

____

How much do you like reading? (check one)
≙ a lot ≙ a little ≙ not at all

How well do you read? (check one)
≙ very well ≙ O.K. ≙ I want to read better

OFFICIAL GUARDIAN MAIL

Mission 31: Update

Dear fellow guardians,

I am impressed by your great form completion skills! And I'm thrilled that I was able to check out the book I requested.

When I turned in my library card form, the head librarian asked if Kirk would be interested in being a reading buddy volunteer. Guess what she gave me? An application Kirk had to fill out. Good thing we learned how to complete forms. Kirk would make a great reading buddy.

I am attaching the solutions to the On Guard section.

Sincerely,

Luke English

Guardian of Grammar Galaxy

Step 1 Solutions

On Guard.

1. The proper noun *New York* would live on which street?
   Person St. **Place St.** Thing St.
2. Which of these is a plural noun?
   running **fines** candy
3. Adjectives tell us:
   which one how where
4. Which word is spelled correctly?
   trusst trest **trust**
5. Writing by hand improves:
   spelling running typing

OFFICIAL GUARDIAN MAIL

Mission 32: Thank-You Notes

Dear guardian friends,

We failed to send a thank-you note to Happy Holographics for the game they sent us and they weren't too happy with us. It turns out that we didn't know how to write a good thank-you note. Our parents helped us and we thought it might be a good idea to share what we learned with you. Please complete this mission and we will let you know how things go with Happy Holographics.

On that note, we hope you know how much we appreciate all your help. We couldn't keep the galaxy running without you. Thank you so much for doing your best on these missions.

Sincerely,

Kirk, Luke, and Ellen English

Guardians of Grammar Galaxy

☆ Step 1: On Guard & Copy the Thank-you note

On Guard. *Add punctuation or letters to correct each of the following sentences.*

1. The king asked, Who sent you the game?

2. Luke exclaimed, "This game is so cool "

3. I have three wish .

4. She ran fast than she did last time.

5. The kids sent a thank-you note to appy olographics.

Say each of these words in a sentence. *Their meanings are given.*

nonetheless – *even so* **immersed** – *engrossed* **quizzical** – *questioning*

Copy the thank-you note. *Write over the thank-you note as quickly as you can, still using good handwriting. Sign your name at the end.*

Dear Happy Holographics,

Thank you so much for the game. We play it all the time. We love your generous gift.

Sincerely,

☆ Step 2: Complete the Fill-in-the-Blank Thank-you note

Fill in the blanks. *Fill in the blanks below for a gift you received (even if it was a while ago or you already sent a thank you).*

Dear

____,

Thank you so much for the

____.

I love it because

____

____.

Love,

____

Activity. *Make a list of people you are thankful for. Get help spelling names if you need it.* ***Hint***: *Think about family members, teachers, coaches, friends, and neighbors. Remember to capitalize names!*

☆ Step 3: Write a Thank-You Letter

Choose a person to thank using the list you made. *Thanking people for helping us, and not just for gifts, is a good practice. Write a letter thanking someone for all they've done for you. Have your teacher help you copy or download the letter on the next page. Use your best handwriting and ask for help with spelling if you need it.* ***Hint:*** *Color in the large letters to make it look even better.*

Vocabulary Victory! *Do you remember what these words mean? Check Step 1 if you forgot.*

nonetheless **immersed** **quizzical**

THANK YOU

Dear ______________________________,

____

____

____

____

____

____

______________________________________.

Love,

____

☆ Advanced Guardians Only

Have your teacher/parent help you address the letter and mail it to the person you thanked, even if it's a family member. *The letter will mean a lot. Your teacher/parent can write on the envelope below and you can copy it to a real envelope.*

OFFICIAL GUARDIAN MAIL

Mission 32: Update

Dear guardian friends,

We are glad to say that Happy Homographics loved our thank-you note. They loved it so much that they said they would send us their newest game when it's ready. We will be sure to write a thank-you note right away when they do!

Writing thank-you notes or letters can make people happy. If you want to make more people happy, write another letter to someone on your list of people you're thankful for. We are attaching the answers to the On Guard section.

Sincerely,

Kirk, Luke, and Ellen English

Guardians of Grammar Galaxy

Step 1 Solutions

On Guard. *Corrections are underlined.*

1. The king asked, "Who sent you the game?"
2. Luke exclaimed, "This game is so cool!"
3. I have three wishes.
4. She ran faster than she did last time.
5. The kids sent a thank-you note to Happy Holographics.

OFFICIAL GUARDIAN MAIL

Mission 33: Directions

Dear guardians,

If you have been trying to follow directions recently, you already know there's a problem. Fire drills have been held in Direction Towers. When the various direction steps tried to return to their respective floors, they got mixed up.

That's where you come in. We need you to put directions back into the right order. We also need you to create some new sets of directions. If you have ideas for other things we can make for Luke for his birthday, we would love it! We so appreciate your help.

Sincerely,

Kirk and Ellen English

Guardians of Grammar Galaxy

☆ Step 1: On Guard & Put Picture Directions in Order

On Guard. *Answer the following questions for your teacher.*

1. What are some story elements or parts you've learned?

2. What's a word that rhymes with bind?

3. What's an antonym for far?

4. What does the contraction wouldn't stand for?

5. What questions does an adverb answer?

Say each of these words in a sentence. *Their meanings are given.*

emanating – *coming* **forbidden** – *not allowed* **mandatory** – *required*

Put picture directions in order. *Write 1, 2, 3, 4, or 5 inside each circle to show how to cook pasta in order.* ***Hint***: *<u>Look carefully at all five pictures first.</u>*

☆ Step 2: Put Steps in Order

List the order of steps below by writing 1-5 next to them. *How do you take a bath in order?* ***Hint***: *Read all the steps before writing.*

_____Dry off with a towel.

_____Plug the drain so the water doesn't run out.

_____Rinse off.

_____Use soap and shampoo.

_____Run the bath water.

Activity. *Make the cupcakes-in-ice-cream-cones recipe the queen and Ellen were making for Luke after putting the steps in the right order, or make another recipe of your choice.*

_____Pour cake batter into paper baking cups & put flat-bottomed ice cream cones upside down into each cup.

_____Eat them.

_____Cool cakes, remove from pan, remove paper baking cups, and frost with icing and sprinkles of your choice.

_____Make cake mix according to directions.

_____Preheat oven to 325 degrees Fahrenheit for dark or nonstick pans or 350 degrees for all other muffin-tin pans.

☆ Step 3: Write Directions

Write directions for something you know how to do that has three steps using the lines below. *Get help spelling if you need it. First write what you are giving directions for after 'How to.'*

How to ______________________________

First, ______________________________

______________________________________.

Then ______________________________

______________________________________.

Finally, ______________________________

______________________________________.

Vocabulary Victory! *Do you remember what these words mean? Check Step 1 if you forgot.*

emanating **forbidden** **mandatory**

☆ Advanced Guardians Only

Write directions for how to make something you think Luke would like for his birthday. *Get help spelling if you need it.*

How to Make ______________________________

1. ______________________________

2. ______________________________

3. ______________________________

4. ______________________________

5. ______________________________

6. ______________________________

OFFICIAL GUARDIAN MAIL

Mission 33: Update

Dear guardians,

Father was able to have future fire drills canceled in Direction Towers. And because you were able to put so many directions back in order, things have been a lot less confusing.

We wanted to especially thank those of you who gave us gift ideas for Luke. He had a great birthday and he loved everything we made!

We are attaching this mission's solutions.

Sincerely,

Kirk and Ellen English

Guardians of Grammar Galaxy

Step 1 Solutions

On Guard.

1. **What are some story elements or parts we've learned?** characters, setting, plot.
2. **What's a word that rhymes with bind?** kind, lined, mind, fined, wind, etc.
3. **What's an antonym for far?** near or close.
4. **What does the contraction wouldn't stand for?** would not.
5. **What questions does an adverb answer?** how, when, where.

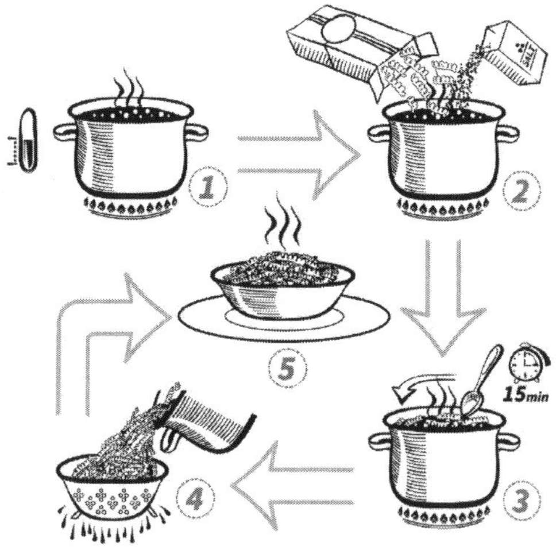

Note: Arrows are not required.

Step 2 Solutions

__5__Dry off with a towel.

__1__Plug the drain so the water doesn't run out.

__4__Rinse off.

__3__Use soap and shampoo.

__2__Run the bath water.

Step 3 Solutions:

__3__Pour cake batter into paper baking cups & put ice cream cones upside down into each cup.

__5__Eat them.

__4__Cool cakes, remove paper baking cups, and frost with icing of your choice.

__2__Make cake mix according to directions.

__1__Preheat oven to 325 degrees Fahrenheit for dark or nonstick pans or 350 degrees for all over muffin tin pans.

OFFICIAL GUARDIAN MAIL

Mission 34: Introductions

Dear fellow guardians,

We would like to introduce ourselves. You know who we are, but we really want to be comfortable introducing ourselves to groups. Ellen had a problem introducing herself to her Grammar Girls group because she had not done it before. Because you are officially guardians of this galaxy, we think it's important for you to be comfortable introducing yourselves too. This mission will help you do that.

Sincerely,

Kirk, Luke, and Ellen English

Guardians of Grammar Galaxy

☆ Step 1: On Guard & Complete the "About Me" Form

On Guard. *Highlight the correct answer for each question.*

1. Which article would come before the word amazing?
   a an

2. Other words and pictures are part of the:
   context adverbs pronouns

3. To find a synonym, you use a:
   homograph thesaurus apatasaurus

4. An exclamation point is an:
   article homograph end mark

5. Which of the following words is a verb?
   runner fast cheated

Say each of these words in a sentence. *Their meanings are given.*

wary – *cautious* **appalling** – *awful* **chagrin** – *irritation*

Complete the "About Me" form. *The form on the next page will help you think about what to say when you introduce yourself.*

ABOUT ME

My name is ____.

I am __________ years old.

I am from / live in____.

I have _________ brothers and sisters.

I have a pet____________________ named____________________.

A sport I like to play is_____________________________________.

An instrument I play is______________________________________.

A hobby I have is____.

My favorite books to read are_________________________________.

My favorite place to go is____________________________________.

My favorite food is____.

My favorite color is____.

A job I would like to have is__________________________________.

Something unique about me is _________________________________

____.

☆ Step 2: Interview Someone

Ask someone the questions in the form below. *We sometimes have to introduce someone else. Write down what a friend, teacher, or family member tells you next to each question.*

Person Interviewed ____

How old are you?____________

Where do you live?____

Have you lived other places?____________________________________

How many brothers and sisters do you have?____________________

Do you have any pets?____

What are your hobbies?____

What are your favorite types of books to read?___________________

____

Where is your favorite place to travel?__________________________

What is your favorite food?______________________________________

What is your job now or what job would you like to have?________

____

What is something unique about you? ____________________________

____

Activity. *Look over the answers and pretend that you are introducing this person to a crowd while the person you interviewed listens. You can use the notes you took to help you as you speak, but try to look up from the paper. You could start with, "I would like to introduce (person's name)." How did the person you interviewed think you did? Take any suggestions and try again.*

☆ Step 3: Introduce Yourself

Review what you will say. *Practice giving a short introduction of yourself with family and friends. Imagine that you are speaking to a group of people you don't know and have been asked to share your: 1)name; 2)age; and 3)something you love to do in your free time. You will want to smile and look people in the eye as you speak. Your introduction might be something like this: "Hi! My name is Alex. I am 10 years old and I love robotics."*

Hint: *Sit up or stand tall. Keep your hands in your lap, clasped in front of you, or at your sides. If you have the chance to practice with people you don't know, even better. The more you practice, the more comfortable you will be.*

Vocabulary Victory! *Do you remember what these words mean? Check Step 1 if you forgot.*

wary **appalling** **chagrin**

☆ Advanced Guardians Only

Practice giving a long introduction of yourself. *Sometimes you will be asked to tell a group about yourself. Review the form you completed in Step 1. What information would a group of people you just met want to know about you?*

When you're ready, have your teacher videotape you. *Watch the video. Did you look relaxed? Did you smile? Did you look at the camera (takes the place of eye contact)? Were you able to speak smoothly? If not, repeat the process until you're satisfied with the results.*

OFFICIAL GUARDIAN MAIL

Mission 34: Update

Dear guardian friends,

Ellen is so happy. She was able to introduce herself at the second Grammar Girls meeting. She told them that she loves to scrapbook and she is learning how to cook. The other girls were very nice about it.

We look forward to hearing you introduce yourselves (or someone else) in the future. We know all your practice will pay off!

We are enclosing the solutions to the On Guard questions.

Sincerely,

Kirk, Luke, and Ellen English

Guardians of Grammar Galaxy

Step 1 Solutions

On Guard.

1. Which article would come before the word amazing?
   a   an
2. Other words and pictures are part of the:
   context   adverbs   pronouns
3. To find a synonym, you use a:
   homograph   thesaurus   apatasaurus
4. An exclamation point is an:
   article   homograph   end mark
5. Which of the following words is a verb?
   runner   fast   cheated

OFFICIAL GUARDIAN MAIL

Mission 35: Reading Aloud

Dear guardians,

Now that you are becoming such good readers, you will want to read aloud for others, whether it's for family or a group. Luke learned that it can be difficult to do without practice. We are sending you a mission that will improve your reading fluency and will help you feel confident reading for others.

Sincerely,

Kirk, Luke, and Ellen English

Guardians of Grammar Galaxy

☆ Step 1: On Guard & Read a Passage Out Loud

On Guard. *Highlight TRUE or FALSE for each statement.*

1. You should stare at the floor when introducing yourself.	TRUE	FALSE
2. Handwriting speed is important.	TRUE	FALSE
3. DOB on a form stands for Date of Bread.	TRUE	FALSE
4. You should write something more than 'thank you' in a note.	TRUE	FALSE
5. Good directions should have steps in order.	TRUE	FALSE

Say each of these words in a sentence. *Their meanings are given.*

empathetic – *sympathetic* **anonymous** – *unknown* **dejected** – *sad*

Read a passage out loud. *Read the following passage out loud without reviewing it first. Have your teacher time you and keep track of how many words you struggle with on the next page. If you can't read a word, skip it and move to the next.*

"I never saw such children," said the old hen. "You don't try at all."

"We can't jump so far, Mother. Indeed, we can't, we can't!" chirped the little chickens.

"Well," said the old hen, "I must give it up." So she jumped back to the bank and walked slowly home with her brood.

"I think Mother asked too much of us," said one little chicken to the others.

"Well, I tried," said Chippy.

"We didn't," said the others; "it was of no use to try."

When they got home, the old hen began to look about for something to eat. She soon found, near the back door, a piece of bread.

So she called the chickens, and they all ran up to her, each one trying to get a bite at the piece of bread.

"No, no!" said the old hen.

"This bread is for Chippy. He is the only one of my children that really tried to jump to the stone."

Passage taken from the McGuffey First Eclectic Reader, Revised Edition, by William Holmes McGuffey; Lesson 62.

Time to Finish Reading Passage________ Reading Errors_________

Note: *You had not read this before, so reading it will take you longer and mistakes are to be expected. You will improve, just as you did with handwriting speed.*

☆ Step 2: Read With Your Teacher

Listen to your teacher read the passage. *Notice how s/he pronounces words and when his or her voice rises and falls. Move your finger underneath each word as it is read.*

"I never saw such children," said the old hen. "You don't try at all."

"We can't jump so far, Mother. Indeed, we can't, we can't!" chirped the little chickens.

"Well," said the old hen, "I must give it up." So she jumped back to the bank and walked slowly home with her brood.

"I think Mother asked too much of us," said one little chicken to the others.

"Well, I tried," said Chippy.

"We didn't," said the others; "it was of no use to try."

When they got home, the old hen began to look about for something to eat. She soon found, near the back door, a piece of bread.

So she called the chickens, and they all ran up to her, each one trying to get a bite at the piece of bread.

"No, no!" said the old hen.

"This bread is for Chippy. He is the only one of my children that really tried to jump to the stone."

Activity. *This time read the passage out loud* *with* *your teacher. Can you keep up? Keep practicing and then read it again by yourself while your teacher times you and tracks errors. Did you improve?*

"I never saw such children," said the old hen. "You don't try at all."

"We can't jump so far, Mother. Indeed, we can't, we can't!" chirped the little chickens.

"Well," said the old hen, "I must give it up." So she jumped back to the bank and walked slowly home with her brood.

"I think Mother asked too much of us," said one little chicken to the others.

"Well, I tried," said Chippy.

"We didn't," said the others; "it was of no use to try."

When they got home, the old hen began to look about for something to eat. She soon found, near the back door, a piece of bread.

So she called the chickens, and they all ran up to her, each one trying to get a bite at the piece of bread.

"No, no!" said the old hen.

"This bread is for Chippy. He is the only one of my children that really tried to jump to the stone."

****

Time to Finish Reading Passage________ Reading Errors__________

☆ Step 3: Read Poetry for Fluency

Complete the same process with a poem. *Read it out loud without reviewing it. Have your teacher time you and track errors. Then have your teacher read it. Read it with your teacher. Practice and then read it while your teacher tracks time and errors again.*

"My Shadow" by Robert Louis Stevenson

I have a little shadow that goes in and out with me,
And what can be the use of him is more than I can see.
He is very, very like me from the heels up to the head;
And I see him jump before me, when I jump into my bed.
The funniest thing about him is the way he likes to grow—
Not at all like proper children, which is always very slow;
For he sometimes shoots up taller like an india-rubber ball,
And he sometimes gets so little that there's none of him at all.
He hasn't got a notion of how children ought to play,
And can only make a fool of me in every sort of way.
He stays so close beside me, he's a coward, you can see;
I'd think shame to stick to nursie as that shadow sticks to me!
One morning, very early, before the sun was up,
I rose and found the shining dew on every buttercup;
But my lazy little shadow, like an arrant sleepy-head,
Had stayed at home behind me and was fast asleep in bed.

****

Note: A *nursie* is a nanny or babysitter; *arrant* means complete; a *buttercup* is a flower.

1st Reading:

Time to Finish Reading Passage________ Reading Errors________

2nd Reading:

Time to Finish Reading Passage________ Reading Errors________

Vocabulary Victory! *Do you remember what these words mean? Check Step 1 if you forgot.*

empathetic **anonymous** **dejected**

☆ Advanced Guardians Only

Choose a story or poem to practice and read aloud for family or a group. *You can also write your own poem to read (like Kirk did) on the lines below. The poem does not have to rhyme.*

OFFICIAL GUARDIAN MAIL

Mission 35: Update

Dear guardians and great readers,

Luke has been working hard on reading aloud and plans to do much better at next year's Poetry Reading Festival. We have heard that you've been working hard too. Way to go! Now any time you are asked to read out loud, you will feel more confident. Keep practicing!

We are attaching the solutions to the On Guard questions.

Sincerely,

Kirk, Luke, and Ellen English

Guardians of Grammar Galaxy

Step 1 Solutions

On Guard.

1.	You should stare at the floor when introducing yourself.	TRUE **FALSE**
2.	Handwriting speed is important.	**TRUE** FALSE
3.	DOB on a form stands for Date of Bread.	TRUE **FALSE**
4.	You should write something more than 'thank you' in a note.	**TRUE** FALSE
5.	Good directions should have steps in order.	**TRUE** FALSE

OFFICIAL GUARDIAN MAIL

Mission 36: Storytelling

Dear guardian friends,

We have a story for you! Luke was asked to tell stories at the library. He thought he just had to read books to younger kids. It turned out that the librarians wanted him to tell stories from memory instead. Luke hadn't done that before, so he felt pretty unprepared. He tried to tell them that, but they didn't seem to understand.

Then Luke tried to tell our father that he couldn't tell stories, but he didn't understand either. Finally, Luke explained the whole thing and it turned out that he was a good storyteller after all! But he was really happy to get some tips on how to be a great storyteller.

He thought (and we agree) that all guardians should learn the art of storytelling. Please complete this mission so Luke won't be the only storyteller at the library.

Sincerely,

Kirk, Luke, and Ellen English

Guardians of Grammar Galaxy

☆ Step 1: On Guard & Memorize the Story and Use Pictures to Tell It

On Guard. *Answer the questions for your teacher.*

1. Why is reading so important?

2. Why is vocabulary important?

3. Why does spelling matter?

4. Why does grammar (the proper use of language) matter?

5. Why does handwriting speed matter?

Say each of these words in a sentence. *Their meanings are given.*

qualified – *able* **flattered** – *praised* **dumbfounded** – *stunned*

Memorize the story and use pictures to tell it. *Ask your teacher to read you "The Tortoise and the Hare" from The Aesop for Children until you know the story. Then use only the pictures on the next page to tell the story to your teacher.* ***Note****: Swift means fast.*

THE HARE AND THE TORTOISE

A Hare was making fun of the Tortoise one day for being so slow.

"Do you ever get anywhere?" he asked with a mocking laugh.

"Yes," replied the Tortoise, "and I get there sooner than you think. I'll run you a race and prove it."

The Hare was much amused at the idea of running a race with the Tortoise, but for the fun of the thing he agreed. So the Fox, who had consented to act as judge, marked the distance and started the runners off.

The Hare was soon far out of sight, and to make the Tortoise feel very deeply how ridiculous it was for him to try a race with a Hare, he lay down beside the course to take a nap until the Tortoise should catch up.

The Tortoise meanwhile kept going slowly but steadily, and, after a time, passed the place where the Hare was sleeping. But the Hare slept on very peacefully; and when at last he did wake up, the Tortoise was near the goal. The Hare now ran his swiftest, but he could not overtake the Tortoise in time.

The race is not always to the swift.

START

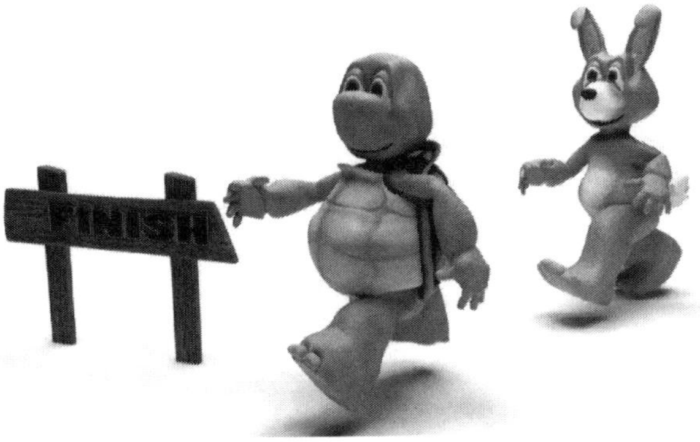
FINISH

☆ Step 2: Tell a Personal or Family Story

Make notes or drawings to help you. *Do you have a favorite story about yourself or a family member? Get help to remember the details if you need it. Make notes or drawings below to help you practice telling it.*

Activity. *Tell your personal or family story to someone who hasn't heard it. How did they like it?*

☆ Step 3: Tell a Favorite Story from a Book

Choose a favorite book and follow the steps from the guidebook. *Tell the story to family or a younger child when you are ready. Use the form below to make notes as you practice.*

Vocabulary Victory! Do you remember what these words mean? Check Step 1 if you forgot.

qualified **flattered** **dumbfounded**

☆ Advanced Guardians Only

Write or dictate your own original story on this page. *Memorize it, practice it, and tell it.*

OFFICIAL GUARDIAN MAIL

Mission 36: Update

Dear storytelling friends,

Luke's first storytelling hour was a big hit! Luke had so much fun telling his story that other kids have volunteered. Maybe now that you've been practicing, you'll want to volunteer to tell stories too.

We are attaching the solution to the On Guard questions for this mission.

If you completed all the missions in the Composition & Speaking Unit, color in or add a sticker to the final star on your Nebula bookmark. If you need more practice, see http://GrammarGalaxyBooks.com/Nebula

We are so proud of you for completing all 36 lessons of the Nebula level. Complete the final challenge we are giving you and you will be ready to move on to the Protostar level.

Sincerely,

Kirk, Luke, and Ellen English

Guardians of Grammar Galaxy

Step 1 Solutions

On Guard.

1.**Why is reading so important?** Because reading helps you succeed in school and life.

2.**Why is vocabulary important?** A good vocabulary also helps you succeed in school and life.

3.**Why does spelling matter?** It prevents confusion.

4.**Why does grammar (the proper use of language) matter?** Good grammar also prevents confusion.

5. **Why does handwriting speed matter?** Writing quickly allows students to take notes and complete written work quickly without getting frustrated. **Note:** *Answers may vary*.

Nebula Final Challenge I

***Carefully read or listen to all the possible answers** and then highlight the letter for the **<u>one</u> best answer**.*

1. If you don't know the meaning of a word, you should look at:

a. any pictures

b. other words in the sentence

c. both pictures and other words in the sentence

2. The following words are synonyms:

a. hot cold

b. small tiny

c. dog cat

3. The following word has a prefix:

a. rewind

b. candy

c. wonderful

4. The following words are in alphabetical order:

a. blue, blind, black

b. fast, first, fix

c. ant, art, arm

5. The following word has three syllables:

a. good

b. better

c. amazing

6. The contraction <u>you're</u> stands for:

a. something that belongs to you

b. you are

c. you were

7. The following is a common and proper noun word pair:

a. boy Rob

b. state capital

c. pet fish

8. The following sentence uses a pronoun:

a. Tracy walked quickly.

b. Ben was a fast runner.

c. I hurt my leg.

9. The following sentence has an adjective and an adverb:

a. The big ship moved slowly.

b. We have one dog.

c. Hawks flew overhead.

10. The following sentence needs quotation marks:

a. She told me where it was.

b. I didn't know, so I asked her.

c. She said, Go left at the stop sign.

Number Correct:________/10

☆ *Extra Challenge*

How many of these vocabulary words can you remember the meaning of?

gaped	**administrator**	**hastily**	**dutifully**
envisioned	**assistance**	**nonetheless**	**immersed**
quizzical	**emanating**	**forbidden**	**mandatory**
wary	**appalling**	**chagrin**	**empathetic**
anonymous	**dejected**	**qualified**	**flattered**
dumbfounded			

Number Correct:________/21

Nebula Final Challenge 1 Answers

1.c; 2.b; 3.a; 4.b; 5.c; 6.b; 7.a; 8.c; 9.a; 10.c

If you got 9 or more correct, congratulations! You've earned your Composition Star. You can color the star or add a sticker to your Grammar Guardian bookmark. You've completed the Nebula level and are ready for the Protostar book. See http://GrammarGalaxyBooks.com for ordering.

If you did not get 9 or more correct, don't worry. You have another chance. You may want to have your teacher review the information from each chapter on the questions you missed. Then take the Nebula Final Challenge 2. Remember to **choose the one best answer**.

Extra Challenge Answers

Here are the meanings of the vocabulary words. Review, say them in a sentence, and see if you can remember more of them.

gaped - *stared*	**administrator** - *manager*	**hastily** – *hurriedly*
dutifully – *obediently*	**envisioned** - *imagined*	**assistance** – *help*
nonetheless – *even so*	**immersed** – *engrossed*	**quizzical** - *questioning*
emanating - *coming*	**forbidden** – *not allowed*	**mandatory** - *required*
wary - *cautious*	**appalling** - *awful*	**chagrin** – *irritation*
empathetic – *sympathetic*	**anonymous** - *unknown*	**dejected** – *sad*
qualified - *able*	**flattered** – *praised*	**dumbfounded** - *stunned*

Nebula Final Challenge 2

***Carefully read or listen to all the possible answers** and then highlight the letter for the **<u>one</u> best answer**.*

1. If you have poor reading comprehension, you can't:

a. spell

b. speak

c. understand

2. What happens in a story is called the:

a. setting

b. plot

c. pronoun

3. Which words rhyme?

a. fin fine

b. mark check

c. fin win

4. When would you use the word <u>best</u> to compare?

a. three people racing

b. two people racing

c. two people writing

5. Which word is a compound word?

a. living room

b. sunroom

c. rooms

6. Which sentence includes an abbreviation?

a. "I am two years old," she said.

b. "I live on Big Bend Road," she said.

c. Mrs. Smith was our teacher.

7. Which word is a correct plural noun?

a. boxs

b. boxes

c. boxis

8. Which word could follow the article <u>an</u>?

a. old

b. red

c. can

9. Which word is a noun?

a. helped

b. small

c. girl

10. Which sentence should end in an exclamation point?

a. I'm so bored

b. Help

c. Can we go home

Number Correct:________/10

Grammar Challenge 2 Answers

1.c; 2.b; 3.c; 4.a; 5.b; 6.c; 7.b; 8.a; 9.c; 10.b

If you got 9 or more correct, congratulations! You've earned your Composition Star. You can color the star or add a sticker to your Grammar Guardian bookmark. You've completed the Nebula level and are ready for the Protostar book. See http://GrammarGalaxyBooks.com for ordering.

If you did not get 9 or more correct, don't worry. Review the questions you missed with your teacher. You may want to get more practice using the resources at http://GrammarGalaxyBooks.com/Nebula. Your teacher can ask you other questions like the ones you missed and if you get them correct, you'll be ready for the Protostar book. See http://GrammarGalaxyBooks.com for ordering.

Made in the USA
Monee, IL
16 June 2024

59446398R00195